GAVIN D SMITH

Whisky Wit & Wisdom

A VERBAL DISTILLATION

Angel's Share

Whisky Wit & Wisdom

Published by The Angel's Share

An imprint of Neil Wilson Publishing Ltd
303a The Pentagon Centre
36 Washington Street
GLASGOW
G3 8AZ

Tel: 0141-221-1117
Fax: 0141-221-5363
E-mail: info@nwp.sol.co.uk
http://www.angelshare.co.uk

A catalogue record for this book is available from the British Library.

ISBN 1-897784-90-2

Typeset in Bembo
Designed by Mark Blackadder
Printed by Interprint, Malta

Contents

For my father, Don, and my late mother,
Lily, who gave me whisky.
It's not their fault if I still lack wit and wisdom.

Acknowledgements

Grateful thanks go to the many individuals who have contributed in various ways to this book, and to those who encouraged its creation. They include Billy Connolly, Ronnie Corbett, Harold Currie, Campbell Evans, Iain Henderson, John Herries, John Hurt, Richard Joynson, Chris McCully, John McDougall, Charles MacLean, Murdo MacDonald, Hugh Morison, Richard Paterson, David Ross, Donald Smith, Ruth Smith, Brian Townsend, Jim Turle and Neil Wilson.

Acknowledgement is also due to the following authors and publishers without whom...Bergius, Adam, *Make Your Own Scotch Whisky* (Argyll Publishing); Bond, Keith, *Memoirs of An Exciseman* (Bond); Chandler, Raymond, *The Big Sleep* and *Farewell, My Lovely* (Hamish Hamilton Ltd); Gunn, Neil M., *Whisky and Scotland* (Routledge & Sons); Harrison Kroll, Harry, *Bluegrass, Belles, and Bourbon* (AS Barnes & Co Inc); Hills, Phillip (Ed.), *Scots on Scotch* (Mainstream Publishing Ltd); MacCaig, Norman, *A Round of Applause* (Chatto & Windus Ltd); The Macallan Distillers Ltd; MacDiarmid, Hugh, *A Drunk Man Looks at the Thistle* (Carcanet Press Ltd);

Preface

'Whisky, no doubt, is a devil, but why has this devil so many worshippers?'
LORD COCKBURN (1779-1854), JUDGE AND MAN OF LETTERS.

'Whisky is the cure for which there is no disease.'

Eighty-four million cases of Scotch whisky were consumed worldwide in 1998. It is the world's best-selling spirit. Apparently, if you laid all those cases end to end they would stretch from Edinburgh to Hong Kong and back again. Personally, I think they should have saved the trouble of measuring, and just stacked them all in my garage.

Scotch sells in more than 200 countries, employs directly more than 12,000 people in Britain, and a further 60,000 indirectly. Annual exports of Scotch whisky are worth £170,000 per employee. It is one of the UK's top five export earners, and also accounts for around 38% of the UK spirits market - more than gin and vodka combined. And that's just the output of one whisky-making nation. Add to that Ireland, USA, Canada, Japan, and all the unusual and unlikely ones, and you can see that whisky is clearly A Serious Business.

Even more serious is the fanaticism of whisky nerds who are prepared to pay the equivalent of a new Vauxhall Astra for an elderly bottle of The Macallan which they don't intend to drink. Nothing in the pages following is funnier than that.

Increasing interest in all aspects of whisky has led to a bewildering range of specialist bottlings of single malts, and the new millennium saw a rash of limited edition efforts, many of which were a triumph of marketing and style over substance. One imaginative – if somewhat elaborate – exception was produced by Glengoyne, who came up with the idea of a bottling, wherein, according to the company 'the ages of the whiskies add up to 2000.' To add a finishing touch, the bottle was presented in a grandfather clock. Only 2,000 were produced, with a price tag of £555. I saw in the millennium with a Timex and a bottle of Famous Grouse, but then I guess I just lack class.

Fascination with the Water Of Life has been reflected in the number of distillery visitor facilities which have sprung up during the past couple of decades, and also in the literature of the subject. According to that most stylish of whisky writers, Charlie MacLean, virtually twice as many English-language whisky books were published in the last decade of the 20th century as had been between 1645 and 1970. Yet still we won't stop writing...

Ironically, for an industry which sets so much marketing store by age, Scotch whisky producers have chosen to make youth their God, spending millions of pounds each year targetting the 18-25 age group, who stubbornly ignore the distillers' blandishments.

John Herries, stillman, mashman, and most things 'man' at the happily re-opened Bladnoch Distillery in Galloway reckoned recently that he had noticed a trend among young drinkers in the area to opt for whisky, especially the females, but perhaps that ostensibly encouraging sign actually says more about Wigtown girls than anything else...

Traditionally, the makers of Scotch have relied heavily on the stock tartan-and-mist clichés to sell their product. Sexism and militarism have also been rife, but such advertising has its downside, too. It does not appeal to the 'yoof'. Personally, I think it's high time that Scotland's distillers made a virtue of the fact that Scotch is primarily a drink for curmudgeonly old farts, and spent their promotion and advertising budget on reducing the price of the stuff for we loyal and committed customers. But then I'm just a curmudgeonly old fart. Whisky shouldn't primarily be about consumer demographics and auction prices. It's not an electrical component or a shelf-bracket; it's a drink created with a great degree of individuality and integrity – a product of its environment, whether it's Kentucky or Speyside. As someone once wrote, 'To drink a glass of Scotch whisky is to drink of the land itself.' Actually, it was me.

Whisky fuels celebrations and provides solace in times of need, and like all alcohol, it occasionally encourages people to cope with the day to day business of simply being alive. The actor John Hurt once said, 'Sometimes life is very difficult to take undiluted,' and fellow 'thesp' Tallulah Bankhead dispensed with the 'sometimes' altogether, drinking two bottles of Old Grand-Dad a day until her death from pneumonia in 1968. The last word she uttered was 'bourbon...'

For most whisky drinkers – including us, by the way – the cratur is consumed for its flavour rather than its effects. We are connoisseurs, not boozers. 'I enjoy a drink. You drink. He is a drunk.'

Whisky is about the very stuff of life and this book is intended to reflect that. The inclusion of any sales figures is purely accidental.

Gavin D. Smith, Perth, January 2000

Sister: 'Why, Charles, you've got raw whisky here!'

Charles: 'Well, it's hardly worth while to bring water. We can always find that as we go along – when we want it'.

Chapter 1

Making it

Making whisky is simple.

As you read this, someone will have a mash on the go in a farm steading in Connemara, an industrial estate unit in Dundee, or even a suburban semi in Solihull. Stranger things have happened.

Almost anyone can do it.

So why all the myths and mystique? Why, as tends to be claimed, can it only be made from barley grown in south-facing fields, using water from a Highland burn once blessed by Bonnie Prince Charlie?

The fact is that while making whisky is comparatively easy, making good whisky is a much trickier business. It is also quite a 'hit and miss' affair, with many variable factors – art as well as science.

It is hardly surprising, therefore, that once a distiller discovers he has made a good dram, he is reluctant to change even the smallest detail in the process of production. At its most extreme, this has led to dents being hammered into new stills to make them exact copies of the worn-out vessels they were replacing.

Linkwood Distillery, near Elgin, was founded in 1821, and

when it was completely rebuilt in 1962 the manager Roderick Mackenzie made sure that the new stills were perfect replicas of their predecessors. He was a fervent believer in the notion that the whole 'micro-climate' in which distilling took place affected the quality of whisky produced, and he even refused to allow the removal of cobwebs from the stillhouse!

In his *Make Your Own Whisky* (1972) Adam Bergius, a descendant of William Teacher, describes how it would be possible to distill at home. Eventually, and not too surprisingly, he reaches the conclusion that making good whisky is best left to the experts, and in particular to those who distill Teacher's Highland Cream! Having reached the stage of producing wash from the fermentation process, Bergius writes 'Some weeks before you should have sent an onion to your plumber and asked him to copy it in copper, and make it big enough to hold this Wash'.

'The character of whisky is determined not by the purity of the spirit manufactured, but by the impurities left in the spirit'. - Major Douglas Mackessack of Glen Grant Distillery, Rothes.

Iain Henderson, manager of Laphroaig Distillery on Islay, maintains that whisky is made from four ingredients. 'Three of them are obvious: water, yeast and barley. The fourth is the secret ingredient: people'.

Of all the factors that influence the location of distilleries, a reliable source of pure water is paramount. A good water supply mattered as much to illicit distillers as it does to today's legal ones, so it is not surprising to discover that many modern distilleries occupy the sites of illicit stills. These include Highland Park on Orkney and Ardbeg on Islay.

In the smuggling days, seclusion was just as significant a factor in determining where distilling took place as having decent water on tap. Glendronach Distillery near Huntly in Aberdeenshire takes its water from local springs. No doubt these were important to the shadowy figures who operated their illegal still on the site prior to Glendronach's formal foundation in 1826, but probably just as important was the local colony of rooks, which made a great deal of noise when anyone approached the still.

Despite all the marketing 'hype' about traditional methods and skills handed own through 75 generations of the same distilling family, the fact is that most distilleries today operate quite differently from the way they would have done even half a century ago. Few plants still make their own malt, many stills are steam-heated rather than coal-fired, and the computer consoles in the still rooms of modern distilleries such as Braeval and Allt-a-Bhainne on Speyside wouldn't disgrace a nuclear power plant.

In his autobiography *Wort, Worms & Washbacks*, John McDougall recalls having to spend Saturday afternoons in the mid-1960s breaking up huge lumps of coal by hand ready to fire the stills for Monday's distillation. And he was a trainee manager! Neil Gunn (*Whisky & Scotland*) provides a suitably poetic description of the labour-intensive production processes of old when he writes of men stripped to the waist, using birch sticks in an attempt to subdue the 'yeast-froth' in the washbacks. 'With the automatic switchers going full speed, I have heard one of those backs rock and roar in a perfect reproduction of a really dirty night at sea'.

It is one of the great joys of malt whisky that no matter how carefully someone might attempt to copy the style of a particular spirit, the results are always appreciably different. Even the most rigorous scientific analysis cannot fully explain why.

Writing of the Speyside whisky capital of Dufftown, Maurice Walsh noted that the town's seven distilleries '...were on one mile of a Highland river. They used the same water, peat, and malt, and the methods of brewing and distillation were identical, yet each spirit had its own individual bouquet. One, the best, mellowed perfectly in seven years; another, the least good, was still liquid fire at the end of ten years'.

The now-demolished Inverness distilleries of Glen Albyn and Glen Mhor are often cited as examples of how two distilleries which were almost identically equipped, situated just 100 yards apart, and used the same malt could produce two very different malt whiskies. Their former owner William Birnie put this down to the fact that each had its own water source, though both drew water from the River Ness.

There is a sign above the door of the Old Fitzgerald bourbon distillery in Louisville, Kentucky, which reads 'No chemists allowed. This is a distillery not a whiskey factory.'

'In these early years of maturing it [the spirit] becomes gawky and angular, an early green adolescence capable of being very self-conscious and horrid between the first marvel of birth and the final round fulness of maturity'.

NEIL GUNN.

American corn whiskey is, by common consent, fairly unsophisticated, and one example, called Georgia Moon, proudly guarantees on its label that the contents is 'less than 30 days old.'

Quill Rose was a noted moonshiner in North Carolina, and when asked in court on one occasion whether ageing improved her corn whiskey Rose replied 'Your Honour has been misinformed. I have kept some for a week one time and I couldn't tell it was a bit better than when it was new and fresh'.

'The common belief that whisky improves with age is true. The older I get, the more I like it'. RONNIE CORBETT.

'I like the whisky old and the women young'. ERROL FLYNN.

'Give me a 42-year-old whisky, Robbie.'

'Oh we've none of that tonight, Mr Mac.'

'Well give me four 8 year olds and a 10 year old.'

From the film *Local Hero*

Ex-sherry casks have long been in great demand for maturing malt whisky, and they have become scarcer as Spanish sherry producers have switched to using plastic drums. Tom Morton (*Spirit of Adventure*) advises against maturing whisky in such vessels. 'You'd then get poncy tasters describing 'a thrilling whiff of polycarbonate, overtones of polythene' when nosing that glass of special single-cask Old Glen Pretentious'.

'Whiskies are capricious, sensitive creatures; they are not to be flung at one another like goats. Rather are they to be compared to fillies which are highly likely to plant iron heels in the belly of the too-forward stallion. They must grow acustomed to one another and, unless they have been carefully chosen, no amount of time will persuade them to live together in amity'.

AENEAS MACDONALD ON BLENDING, *WHISKY* (1930).

'Distilling is a science and blending is an art'.

SAMUEL BRONFMANN.

Until the 1980s, all processes of whisky production and storage were overseen by on-site excise officers, but today the uniformed figure of the exciseman is no longer a familiar sight in distilleries, as a policy of self-policing or 'trader control' now prevails.

The Highland author Neil M Gunn was a close friend of the Kerry-born popular novelist Maurice Walsh, who, like Gunn, worked for the excise service before turning to full-time writing. They first met just before the start of the First World War. Gunn was a young 'Unattached Officer', substituting at distilleries all over Scotland for excisemen who were on leave.

Walsh was based at Dallas Dhu, near Forres, on Speyside for a time, and as Gunn put it, 'I'd write ahead and say, "Look here! I'm coming to replace you. Kindly see that the books all are in perfect order so that there is absolutely no work to be done.' The pair would then spend a couple of weeks hunting and fishing together.

Such episodes were to have a place in Walsh's first novel *The Key Above the Door* (1926). The character Neil Quinn writes to his friend Tom King from Skye to inform him that he is spending a month standing on for the resident officer at a distillery which is obviously based on Talisker. '...above all there is the whisky, - Uiskavagh whisky, the finest whisky in the world when drunk in Skye; old as a grown man, mild as your goat's milk, soothing as a woman's hand in your hair, inspiring as a tune − a very great whisky'.

The life of a distillery-based excise officer allowed for a considerable amount of what might today be termed 'flexi-time', with Gunn spending many afternoons at home in Inverness writing novels, while based at the town's now demolished Glen Mhor Distillery. RJS McDowall notes in *The Whiskies of Scotland* that the excise officer is really much busier with his duties than might sometimes seem to be the case, though he adds '...I must confess that I have been to a distillery where the warehouse was wide open and the Excise officer was nowhere to be seen. When I remarked on this I was told, "He trusts us. Maybe he's at the fishing but he keeps wonderful books".'

Former distillery manager John McDougall (*Worts, Worms and Washbacks*) observes that it was not unknown for the gamekeeper to turn poacher.

    'Dailuaine's second excise officer was Ray Lyons, who was extremely good at his job, but who took a serious bucket. He habitually brought his dog to work with him; an Irish Wolfhound called Seamus. He always arrived early in the morning to take the whisky charge and take account of the spirit. Eventually I realised that he arrived early so that he could put the new spirit into the coffee he brought in a flask. As the day wore on the sample tube kept being emptied, Ray's eyes became more glazed and his glasses slid further and further down his nose. Eventually he would call for Seamus, and it became obvious why he brought the dog to work. He needed something to hang onto on the steep path from the distillery up to his house'.

Not all whisky-drinking by excise officers took place on the premises. One officer on Speyside had a pronounced limp, and it was only after he had spent fifteen years at a distillery that the plant's manager saw him by chance one day walking perfectly normally in a town some miles from home. It transpired that the exciseman concealed a metal pipe down his left trouser leg, regularly filling it with whisky during his working days.

One of the most interesting and controversial figures to have been on the payroll of HM Customs & Excise service was John McNachtane, a Highland chief and founder, in 1732, of the 'Beggars Bennison' society. The membership of this society included a number of aristocrats, at least one bishop, fellow customs officers, and even a smattering of smugglers. The society met annually at an inn in the Fife port of Anstruther, and was dedicated to general debuchery, but in particular to what might politely be termed the pleasures of sexual self-gratification. One of the society's prized artefacts was a silver snuff box which had been donated by King George IV, containing samples of pubic hair from his various mistresses. A 'bennison' was a blessing, and the society took its name from a story that King Charles II was once saved from drowning by a beggar woman. It is thought that his thanks took an extremely personal form.

'Ferintosh' whisky had the unique distinction of being distilled without the requirement to pay excise duty between the years of 1690 and 1784. Legend has it that Bonnie Prince Charlie drowned his sorrows after his defeat at the battle of Culloden in 1746 in Ferintosh, and the whisky was distilled locally by Duncan Forbes, enjoying a very high reputation.

Forbes was a staunch supporter of the Protestant King William III, who deposed the Catholic James II in 1688, and his estates were badly damaged during the Jacobite rising in favour of James the following year. £4,500 worth of damage was done to Ferintosh Distillery in the process, and by way of compensation, the Scottish parliament granted Forbes the right to distill at Ferintosh free of duty in perpetuity on payment of 400 marks Scots per year. During the ensuing century while this exemption was in force the Forbes family became very wealthy.

When new excise legislation was introduced in 1784 the 'perk' ended, and the Forbes' were awarded £21,580 in compensation. Robert Burns, for one, was outraged by the ending of the Ferintosh privilege, and his poem *Scotch Drink* (1785) and *The Author's Earnest Cry and Prayer* of the following year articulate his feelings at the loss of Ferintosh's unique status in particular, and the repressive state of the excise laws relating to whisky in general:

> Thee, Ferintosh! Oh, sadly lost!
> Scotland lament frae coast tae coast!
> Now colic grips, an' barkin' hoast
>   May kill us a';
> For loyal Forbes's charter'd boast
>   Is ta'en awa!
> Thae curst horse-leeches o' th' Excise,
> Wha mak the whisky stells their prize!
> Haud up thy han', Deil! ance, twice, thrice!
>   There, seize the blinkers!
> An' bake them up in brunstane pies
>   For poor damn'd drinkers.

Somewhat surprisingly, Burns served as a Dumfries-based excise officer from 1789 until his death in 1796, and wrote what was to become the best-known song about that particular profession. *The Deil's Awa Wi' The Exciseman* was penned in 1792, reputedly while hiding in a salt-marsh on the Solway Firth, keeping a brig suspected of smuggling under surveillance...

> The deil's awa', the deil's awa',
> The deil's awa' wi' the Exciseman;
> He's danced awa', he's danced awa',
> He's danced awa' wi' the Exciseman!

'Dramming' was theoretically illegal, but excise officers usually turned a blind eye to the practice. It consisted of regularly supplying the distillery workforce with glasses of whisky which they drank while on duty. The size of the drams and the frequency with which they were distributed depended on the brewer and the distillery manager, and there was a tradition that very dirty and unpleasant jobs were rewarded with an extra dram. Drink-driving legislation and Health and Safety regulations finally brought an end to the custom.

In the days of dramming, old distillery workers would be known as 'hoggiemen', because they had been plied with the equivalent of a hogshead (55 gallons/250 litres) of whisky during their working lives. One or two extremely well-preserved – or pickled – old retainers even qualified as 'two-hoggiemen'.

Neil Gunn wrote, tongue-in-cheek, 'I have heard a few sad stories of hard-working men of eighty odd winters who were so disheartened by the official edict of abstinence that they gave up their distillery jobs and shortly after died.'

It was not uncommon for distillery workers to want more than their allocated drams, and many ingenious ways were found to smuggle spirit out of the site. Rubber hot water bottles would be filled with whisky and strapped around workers' waists beneath their coats, or copper tubes – known as dogs – would be filled and secreted down trouser legs or the sides of wellington boots. If the spirited-away spirit was for purely personal consumption, the smuggler might escape detection for a considerable length of time, but if, as often happened, it was offered for sale in pubs, then the excise service's intelligence network usually got to hear about it, and retribution was swift and sharp.

In some cases, workers drank wash from the washbacks, claiming it to be an excellent hangover cure. Tom Morton (*Spirit of Adventure*) notes 'as they are almost certainly hopeless alcoholics, this advice should be ignored'.

In his entertaining account of his time in the excise service, *Memoirs of an Exciseman*, Keith Bond writes of distillery workers drinking clearic – the raw, new, high-strength spirit off the stills. He warns that this practice 'renders anyone not used to it insensible practically on the spot. And taking as much as a glass of water for days afterwards causes you to fall maudlin' drunk again instantly'.

It was not unknown for distillery workers to pour boiling water into empty casks in order to draw out the last vestiges of whisky which remained and take this for their private use. The practice was known as 'grogging the cask'. A modern equivalent occurred at a Glasgow bottling plant, where the cardboard-like baffles used during filtering were taken home by workers who ran them through the spin dryers of their washing machines to achieve the same result.

The threat of fires was, and remains, a serious one for distilleries, especially where large quantities of spirit are matured in warehouses on the premises. Several famous Scottish distilleries feature major fires in their histories, including Talisker, Dalwhinnie, Strathisla and Glenmorangie. In the USA, the Heaven Hill Distillery at Bardstown in Kentucky was destroyed by fire in November 1996. Some 90,000 casks of spirit were lost in the blaze.

Perhaps the most bizarre distillery fire occured at Banff on 16 August 1941, when a lone German bomber, perhaps unable to find the docks at Aberdeen, scored a direct hit on one of the warehouses. In the ensuing conflagration casks of spirit were opened and the contents poured into nearby watercourses to prevent the fire spreading. According to the '...thousands of gallons of whisky were lost, either by burning or running to waste over the land...and so overpowering were the results that even farm animals grazing in the neighbourhood became visibly intoxicated.' It is said that none of the local cattle could stand up to be milked the following morning, and one enterprising fireman filled his helmet with whisky as it flowed by, and shared it with his colleagues. Sadly, he ended up in court for his trouble.

The business of making whisky had its lighter moments, as recalled by John McDougall, who, in 1966 was appointed assistant manager of Dailuaine Distillery, near Aberlour-on-Spey. At that time many distilleries still relied on railways for much of their transportation, and Dailuaine was no exception, being served by a 'spur' from the Strathspey Railway line. The distillery boasted its own 'puggie' engine, operated by Willie Wilson, known to one and all as 'Puggie Wul'.

'The puggie engine was quite a feature of Dailuaine, and we even got trainspotters coming to photograph it from time to time. One day we were approached by a French magazine we had never heard of called *Lui*, who wanted to use the engine in a photo shoot with some fashion models. I was put in charge of organising the event, and Puggie Wul got the engine all polished up for the day. The crew duly turned up with the girls wearing full-length fur coats on what I thought was quite a mild day. Soft French lassies, I thought. "Are you wearing those coats because you're feeling the cold?" I asked one of them who had climbed onto the front of the engine. She smiled at me and then pulled her coat open to reveal that she was completely naked underneath. The girls from the distillery office thought this was absolutely disgusting and went and locked themselves in their office. As they were retreating, I noted that the men were leaving their posts in great haste, abandoning the stillhouse, the maltings, the dried solubles plant and every other bit of the distillery to come and watch.

'Geordie Davidson, who worked in the cooperage, was so excited by this turn of events that he pulled a cask from the bottom of the pile in error, and the rest of the heap rolled all over the yard. A few even ended up in the burn and found their way into the Spey.

'My wife chose that precise moment to walk into the yard to

see what all the fuss was about. My protestations that nobody had told me that Lui was that sort of publication were clearly not believed. There were some long silences at home that evening. This was the swinging sixties, but not much was swinging around the Aberlour area – at least not until that day – so the excitement and outrage (according to gender) was not surprising. A while after all this happened, we did get to see the published photographs in *Lui*, and I have to admit it was quite a good feature. When we showed the pictures to Puggie Wul he studied them carefully for a while, then said "Aye, the engine looks well, right enough".

One of the most unusual Scotch whiskies must surely be the blend Hamashkeh, which is a Kosher whisky, produced to the stringent demands of Jewish dietary law. Hamashkeh is made by JBB (Greater Europe) Plc at their Invergordon Distillery, and a Rabbi is present to guarantee that casks used in maturation have not previously contained sherry and even that cleaning fluids used on the premises are acceptable to would-be imbibers.

Glengoyne Distillery near Killearn, a few miles north of Glasgow, is classified as a Highland malt, as the distillery lies just north of the theoretical Highland Line that runs from Greenock in the west to Dundee in the east. Once made, however, the spirit matures in the Lowlands, as Glengoyne's bonded warehouses are across the A81 road from the main distillery, on the other side of the Highland Line!

At Glengoyne the 2% per annum of maturing spirit which generally evaporates into the air amounts to the equivalent of some 100,000 bottles. This is known as the 'angels' share', and is a boon to distillery tour guides, who are guaranteed a laugh from their audiences when they say something like 'no wonder the Highland air is so often described as intoxicating'.

One tour guide at Blair Athol Distillery in Pitlochry is fond of pointing out that when it rains some of the evaporating spirit returns to earth. 'Round about these warehouses', he says, 'the grass comes up already half-cut'.

Glenturret in Perthshire has a place in the *Guinness Book of Records*, thanks to the epic mousing abilities of the distillery's cat, Towser. Towser lived in the stillhouse from 1963 until her death in 1987, and during that time she allegedly accounted for no fewer than 28,899 mice, making her World Mousing Champion. Towser is undoubtedly an excellent marketing tool for Glenturret, having her very own statue outside the visitor centre and being the subject of limited edition ceramic figures. Nobody at Glenturret dwells on who had to count all the corpses.

Towser is not the only distillery cat to have found fame. One day in 1993 a young Kentucky cat from Louisville was inadvertently loaded into a container for shipping along with a consignment of bourbon casks, bound for Keith on Speyside. A month later, on Speyside, a noise was heard coming from the container as Seagram workers unloading the casks discovered a very weak and extremely drunk cat among the barrels. Seagram paid his quarantine bills and subsequently 'employed' him in their Keith bonding complex. Appropriately, they christened him Dizzy.

Glenlivet is one of the most famous names in whisky history. The glen was a notable centre for illicit distillation during the eighteenth and early nineteenth centuries, and now produces one of the best-known and most highly-regarded single malts in existence. The Glenlivet name had a cache about it by the late nineteenth century, when so many distilleries in the area used 'Glenlivet' alongside their own names on the pretext of geographical or stylistic similarity that it jokingly became known as 'the longest glen in Scotland'. Legal action by the Smith family who owned The Glenlivet Distillery led to the situation where other distillers were only allowed to use 'Glenlivet' as a hyphenated addition on their labels. Even Edradour Distillery near Pitlochry got in on the act, at one time being marketed as Glenforres-Glenlivet, despite the distillery being located at least eighty miles as the sober crow flies from the famous Banffshire glen.

Glenlivet it has castles three,
Drumin, Blairfindy and Deskie,
And also one distillery
More famous than the castles three.

ANON.

Freemasons! to the Major drink –
We daurna speak, but we can wink,
An' heaven be thankit, we can think,
An' thinkin', feel richt frisky, O!
Lang may they thrive in stock an' store,
Balmenach, Craggan an' Minmore,
An' I'll be up to ha'e a splore
In gran' Glenlivet Whisky, O!

JAMES SCOTT SKINNER, THE 'STRATHSPEY KING'.

Along with The Glenlivet, Glenfiddich is one of the best-known Speyside single malt whiskies. Glenfiddich Distillery in Dufftown remains in the hands of its founders, Wm Grant & Sons Ltd, and the company is notable for having developed the first distillery visitor centre during the 1960s, as wel as pioneering single malt sales. Glenfiddich is still the best-selling single malt both in Britain and abroad.

The Glenfiddich Distillery was built by William Grant and operated with the help of three of his sons, George, Charlie and Alec. When the Supervisor of the Inland Revenue first visited the distillery after its opening in 1887 he was surprised to find Latin and mathematical text books lying around the plant. He was even more perplexed when told that they belonged to the maltman, the tun room man and the stillman. These were the three Grant boys.

> Lord grant gude luck to a' the Grants,
> Likewise eternal bliss;
> For they should sit amang the sa'nts
> That mak a dram like this.

ANON.

Another Speyside whisky-making Grant, though no relation, was James Grant of Glen Grant Distillery in Rothes. He was universally known as The Major, and travelled extensively in India and Africa, finding an abandoned Matabele boy on an African hunting expedition in 1898. He brought the boy back to Speyside, sent him to school, and subsequently made him his butler. His name was Biawa Makalanga, but he was known as 'Byeway' around Rothes, as the exotic African name eluded most locals. Grant was a formidable fisherman, and at the age of 74 he once caught 38 salmon in a single fishing expedition.

Campbeltown – on the remote Kintyre peninsula – became the largest centre for whisky-making in Scotland during the nineteenth century, and distilling is recorded as having taken place at more than 30 locations in the town. The advent of Prohibition in the USA (1919–1933) led many Campbeltown distillers to produce large quantities of low quality whisky to satisfy the voracious appetite of the illegal speakeasies of American cities, and the overall reputation of Campbeltown whiskies began to suffer during the 1920s. One observer described them as 'stinking fish'.

The proprietors of the town's largest distillery, Hazelburn, tried to get round the problem by writing to its customers to announce that it was no longer making Campbeltown whisky, but was now producing Kintyre whisky. Similarly, Glen Nevis and Springbank magically began to distil 'West Highland' whisky. Nobody was fooled, however, and Hazelburn closed in 1925, two years after Glen Nevis. Today Springbank is one of only two distilleries remaining in Campbeltown.

Campbeltown Loch, I wish you were Whisky,
Campbeltown Loch, Och Aye!
Campbeltown Loch, I wish you were Whisky,
I would drink you dry!

Bessie Williamson became the first woman to own a Scottish distillery, inheriting Laphroaig on the island of Islay from Iain Hunter in 1954. She was already intimately involved in the practical business of distilling, having joined the staff of Laphroaig in 1933 as a temporary shorthand secretary, ultimately becoming Hunter's assistant. She died in 1982, having sold Laphroaig to Long John International during the 1960s.

The story of the rise of a Glaswegian shorthand typist to become a distillery matriarch is so fascinating that few writers spoil the tale by pointing out that Bessie Williamson actually had a degree in pharmacy from Glasgow University, and that her typing career had only come about because jobs for female pharmacists were in short supply during the early 1930s.

The assertive malts made on the southern shores of the island of Islay are among the most distinctive in the world. Their devotees tend to love them with a passion greater than that for any human being.

Laphroaig makes a virtue of the 'love it or hate it' attitude to its malt in its advertising, and along with near neighbour Lagavulin, it is one of those drinks which rarely meets with indifference.

'I loved kissing a smoker. It was like drinking Laphroaig.'

TOM MORTON, *GUTTERED.*

'A liquid kipper' is one description of Lagavulin, and in a *Whisky Magazine* feature about what to eat with whisky Brian Hennigan admitted (brave man) that he favoured Lagavulin and Hula-Hoops. In a 1999 *Scotsman* 'survey' of his attitudes to 'Heaven and Hell', Tony Reekie, Director of the Scottish International Children's Festival,

Making it — 21

responded to the question 'Anything else to declare?' by replying 'Two million packs of Camel Lights and a billion-litre bottle of Lagavulin'. At least he was being health-conscious – he could have chosen regular strength Camels.

That indefatigable chronicler of Victorian distilleries Alfred Barnard allows a rare moment of – perhaps unconscious – humour to creep into his narrative when writing of a visit to Caol Ila, spectacularly located on the north-eastern coast of Islay:

'We soon came in sight of the Distillery lying directly beneath us, and we wonder for a moment how we are to get down to it. Our driver, however, knew the road well, for often had he been here before, and turning sharp to the right, we commenced the descent through a little hamlet of houses. But the way is so steep, and our nerves none of the best, that we insist upon doing the remainder of the descent on foot, much to the disgust of the driver, who muttered strange words in Gaelic. His remarks, however, are lost upon us, that language not having formed part of our education.'

THE WHISKY DISTILLERIES OF THE UNITED KINGDOM (1887)

The origins of distilling are lost in the mists of time, with the Arabs usually being credited with discovering the art of distillation, or at the very least perfecting it, and it is believed to have been brought to Europe in the tenth century by the Moors. Words like 'claim', 'believed' and 'probable' litter all writing on the early history of distilling, because there are so few written records.

There are several Irish references to 'aqua vitae' in the 13th century, and it is claimed – without any foundation in fact – that in 1276 Sir Robert Savage of Bushmills fortified his troops before battle against the native Irish with aqua vitae.

Samuel Morewood (*History of Inebriating Liquors*, 1838) writes of Ireland that '...the English, shortly after the invasion, in the time of Henry II, found the people indulging in potations of this liquour...it is more than probable that it was known in Ireland before the English were acquainted with it.' Or the Scots, he might have added.

Morewood notes that distilling spirit was carried out in monasteries, and that 'the dissoultion of the monasteries gave the secret of this invention to the public, and the elixir of the alembic soon attained the summit of popular regard'.

A beacon of factual light shines in the late fifteenth century, because in the Scottish Exchequer Rolls of 1494 there is the entry '...eight bolls of malt wherewith to make aqua vitae'. If those words sound familiar it's because every whisky writer quotes them in triumph, having finally pinned something down to a specific date.

Eight bolls is 1,20lbs, or 508kgs – a sufficiently large quantity of malt to suggest that whisky-making was already well-established in Scotland by 1494, but again we are into the territory of supposition, so let's leave it at that.

Harold Currie, former Managing Director of Chivas Brothers and the man who created the Isle of Arran Distillery in the mid 1990s, tells the story, tongue-in-cheek, of how he believes that the Irish did, indeed, discover the secret of whisky-making, and that the Scots found them using it as horse linament. The Scots took away the secret, says Currie, and refined it until they came up with the perfect product we have today. The Irish haven't really changed theirs...

'The Irish sort is particularly distinguished for its pleasant and mild flavour. The Highland sort is somewhat hotter...'
DR SAMUEL JOHNSON ON WHISKY IN HIS *DICTIONARY* OF 1755.

It may be difficult to believe today, but there was a time when Irish whiskey was a far more popular drink in Britain than Scotch, and, indeed, was the second most popular spirit in the western world, with sales only being outstripped by rum. This was just before the innovation of blended Scotch whisky began to take the world by storm. One Scots company estimated in 1878 that Dublin whiskey – the creme de la creme of Irish spirit – was selling five times the amount that Scotch was in Britain, and when prohibition was enacted in the USA there were some 400 brands of 'Irish' on sale in North America. Prohibition was a very serious blow to the Irish distillers, while the 'War of Independence' (1919-21) and the subsequent trade war with Britain denied them access to English and Empire markets. The Scottish blenders were not slow to take advantage.

Ireland currently boasts just three working distilleries, at Bushmills in County Antrim, Cooley in County Louth, and Midleton in Cork, but when Alfred Barnard visited Ireland in 1886, he toured no fewer than 28 distilleries. Jerome K Jerome's popular comic novel *Three Men in a Boat* was published three years after Barnard's trip across the Irish Sea, and in it the character Harris talks of a Thames public house '...where you could get a drop of Irish worth drinking'.

Whiskey was made in the Londonderry town of Coleraine from 1820 until 1978, and Coleraine was one of the few Irish distilleries to have marketed pure malt whiskey. A Tipperary-born Coleraine school master by the name of James Feehan celebrated Coleraine whiskey in a song which begins:

> The Spaniard may boast of his sherry
> The Frenchman his sparkling champagne,
> But if a man wants to be merry,
> I'd advise him to try 'Old Coleraine'.

> You may search in the annals of history
> To the time of the Roman and Dane
> But you'll find it was reckoned a mystery,
> How they made such good stuff in Coleraine.

> *Chorus*
> Then hurrah! for the 'trim little borough'
> And the Bann as it flows through the plain;
> Its waters will banish all sorrow
> When mixed with a drop of 'Coleraine'.

One of the most evocative names in American distilling is that of Jack Daniels, and the Jack Daniels Distillery at Lynchburg in Tennessee is the most visited distillery in the world, welcoming more than 300,000 members of the public per year. Sadly, however, the operators do not offer visitors a dram at the end of their tours as is customary in Scotland. This is not due to parsimony, rather to the fact that Lynchburg is located in a 'dry' county.

Jack Daniels learnt the art of distilling at the age of just seven from a Lutheran pastor by the name of Dan Call. When Jack was 13 years old, Call sold him his distillery, as a result of pressure from his church, which considered distilling to be incompatible with his ecclesiastical standing. Clearly no such obstacles had existed for the Rev Elijah Craig, who is credited with accidentally discovering the cask charring process which gives bourbon its distinctive characteristics in 1789, when a fire damaged his cask store.

Daniels died in 1911, and his death is perhaps more bizarre than that of fellow distillers who tumbled into vats of wash or burnt ale. He stubbed his toe on an office safe, and, despite a number of amputations, eventually died of the injury.

Despite the world-wide fame of Jack Daniels, the heart of modern American distilling lies in the state of Kentucky. As Harry Harrison Kroll notes in his 1967 book *Bluegrass, Belles, and Bourbon*, 'Kentucky distills 70 per cent of all the straight and bonded whiskies in the United States. It's been the homeland of whisky making, licit and illicit, from the beginning'.

Kroll opens his highly entertaining study of Kentucky distilling with the following offering:

STRANGER (passing through Kentucky): 'I know something about bourbon and belles, but what the hell's the bluegrass got to do with it?'

OLD RESIDENTER (well in his cups): 'Suh, you and the belle drinks the bourbon, and then you lays the belle in the bluegrass, heh-heh-heh!'

Kroll recalls his first impression of the whiskey-making centre of Bardstown '...was that of a bone-dry oasis completely surrounded by whiskey distilleries and statues of Abe Lincoln.

'Or farms where Abe once lived. Or motels – ah, the motels, $7 and up single in the tourist season – where Abe once trod as a lad, or yokel, or a candidate for statues. If the motel builders couldn't find a farm where old man Lincoln once lived, they quarried rocks from a neighboring farm to build the motels. Since such quarters were of low status in sentimental and historical associations, the beginning rate was $6 single'.

In a statement that now seems just as appropriate to some parts of the Scottish Highlands, Kroll wrote more than 30 years ago that 'Bardstown lives off tourists and whisky distilleries'.

'A man to get on in this business eats, drinks, sleeps, reads, lives liquor'
SAM CECIL, VICE-PRESIDENT OF STAR HILL DISTILLERY,
LORETTO, KENTUCKY. HOME OF MAKER'S MARK WHISKEY. (1966).

Lincoln Henderson is master distiller for Brown-Forman in Louisville, Kentucky, where he is involved with such famous bourbons as Jack Daniel and Early Times, not to mention Southern Comfort. When asked by his teacher what his father did for a living, Henderson's young son replied 'He's a whiskey-taster and he drinks nine quarts of whiskey a day'.

First North Briton (on the Oban boat, in a rolling sea and dirty weather):

'Thraw it up, man, and ye'll feel a' the better'

Second ditto (keeping it down): 'Hech mon, it's whuskey!!'

Chapter 2
Drinking it

'Moderation is my rule. Nine or ten is reasonable refreshment, but after that it's apt to degenerate into drinking'.

ANONYMOUS IMBIBER IN AN ANGUS BAR.

Most of the best 'occasional' whisky-drinking stories seem to concern funerals (see chapter 6), but the following is a wedding-related tale, told by my father.

'We went to a Caithness fishing village to visit some relatives one day in the late 1950s. On arrival in the village just before lunchtime on a Thursday it soon became obvious that not one adult was even remotely sober.

'We were greeted with extreme enthusiasm by my uncle and aunt, taken into the house, and plied with repeated tumblers half-filled with suspiciously clear whisky of an extraordinary strength. Another relative worked at the Pulteney Distillery in Wick, which may not have been coincidental.

'As I was driving, I began surreptitiously to tip the spirit into a handily-placed aspidistra plant, once the ham on my plate appeared to be spinning out of control as I tried to spear it with my fork.

'Mention was made of Seona's wedding, and we assumed that it had just taken place. "No, no," said Uncle Danny, "the weddin's no' till Saturday, we've a' just been doon tae the hall tae look at the presents."

'The Whisky of this country is a most rascally liquor; and by consequence, only drunk by the most rascally part of the inhabitants'.
ROBERT BURNS IN A LETTER OF 22ND DECEMBER 1788.

The word 'country' refers to the area around Dumfries. At the time, Burns was living at Ellisland Farm, a few miles from the town.

The writer Albert Mackie considered that the perfect Scottish breakfast consisted of a bottle of whisky, a haggis and a collie dog. When asked the purpose of the collie, Mackie replied 'to eat the haggis'.

The English angler offered his Highland ghillie a very modest glass of whisky by the riverside after a long morning's fishing. MacDonald, the ghillie, looked less than excited by his dram.

'What's the matter with it, MacDonald?', queried the angler, 'it's a twelve year old'.

'Well', replied MacDonald, 'it's awfu' small for its age'.

Queen Victoria enjoyed whisky, and was once observed by Prime Minister Gladstone pouring a measure of it into a glass of claret she was drinking. Her devoted ghillie John Brown enjoyed whisky on a copious scale, but her majesty indulged him in this. On one occasion at Balmoral, an inebriated Brown stumbled and fell over in front of Victoria. Undismayed, the queen announced to the assembled company that she too had felt an earth tremor.

Whisky has often been used – or wasted, depending on one's point of view – on animals. It is thought that early Christian monks in Egypt used alcohol as a rub for the stiff legs of mules, later applying the same treatment to humans. Just when this external therapy switched to internal therapy is a matter for scholarly debate. That is to say, nobody actually knows.

The former West Cork racehorse trainer Fergie Sutherland used to rub illegally distilled poitin into the legs of 1986 Cheltenham Gold Cup winner Imperial Call after exercise.

An Irish farmer, Jerome O'Leary, owned the world's oldest cow, Big Bertha, who died in 1994 at the age of fifty. Jerome insisted that her longevity was due to the fact that after attending fund-raising events the pair would stop off at a pub on the way home and Bertha would be given some Guinness or whiskey.

During an Irish court case concerning poitin in January 1977 Mr Justice O'Farrell said 'I hear it's a great rub for the lumbago'.

According to John McGuffin in *In Praise of Poteen*, 'The

practice had been common for years of selling off 'singlings', the first run, which is harsh, very strong and almost undrinkable, to people suffering from sprains, hacks and cuts.'

The singlings also made nutritious, and very palatable, cattle feed. As McGuffin reports '...in 1854 it was said that a man bringing a cow in peak condition to a Donegal fair was automatically suspected of illicit distillation, and the practice of feeding singlings to cattle continues to this day.'

The Japanese have been known to use whisky as an embrocation for cattle, as it is reckoned to make the resultant leather more supple.

The origin of the expression 'a drop of the herd stuff'?

Robin Browning, chief executive of the British Linen Bank, recalled in a speech being dispatched to take charge of the Bank of Scotland branch in Errol, Perthshire. Being a diligent young man he decided on his first morning to check that the bank alarm was in working order. Browning pressed the button threee times, and was greeted by three loud rings, which suggested that all was well. All became even better, however, when a waiter appeared from a nearby hotel bearing three glasses of whisky on a tray.

'There's some takes delight in the carriages a-rollin',
And others take delight in the hurley and the bowlin',
But I take delight in the juice of the barley,

And courtin' pretty fair maids in the

mornin' bright and early...'

FROM WHISKEY IN THE JAR (TRAD.).

To add water, or not to add water.

Predicably, there are two schools of thought, both convinced their view is correct. A little clean water certainly helps to release the bouquet of a decent malt, and a cask-strength malt is almost undrinkable without being reduced.

There is scope, however, for dispute, even between the devotees of dilution. The purists favour spring water, ideally from the same source as the water used in the whisky's production. The pragmatists consider any decent tap water that is not overly chlorinated and has not previously been through too many sets of kidneys to be acceptable. As is so often the case, we have been blessed with a wise Celtic utterance on the matter: 'There are two things a Highlander likes naked, and one is his whisky'.

Continuing with the politically incorrect, the following is a Gaelic toast in praise of whisky:

<table>
<tr><td>Is coisiche na h-oidhche thu</td><td>You are the prowler of the night</td></tr>
<tr><td>Gu leapannan na maighdeannan;</td><td>To the beds of virgins;</td></tr>
<tr><td>A Righ! gur h-iomadh loinn a th'ort</td><td>O God! what powers you have</td></tr>
<tr><td>Gu coibhneas thoirt a gruagach.</td><td>To gain kindness from girls.</td></tr>
</table>

'Whisky suffers its worst insults at the hands of the swillers, the drinkers-to-get-drunk who have not organs of taste and smell in them but only gauges of alcoholic content, the boozers, the 'let's-have-a-spot' and 'make-it-a-quick-one' gentry, and all the rest who dwell in a darkness where there are no whiskies but only whisky – and, of course, soda.'

AENEAS MACDONALD, *WHISKY*.

'As an instance of acute hydrophobia, it is difficult to surpass the story of the boatman who, while crossing a loch, was asked if he would take some water with his whisky, and replied, "Na, there was a horse drooned at the heid o' the loch twa years ago." The head of the loch was twenty-four miles distant.'

WILLIAM HARVEY, *SCOTTISH LIFE & CHARACTER* (1899).

It's all mighty fine what Taytotallers say,
'That you're not to go drinking of sperits,
But to keep to pump wather, and gruel, and tay' –
Faith, ye'd soon have a face like a ferret's.
I don't care one sthraw what such swaddlers may think,
(ye'll find them in every quarther),
The wholesomest liquor in life you can dhrink,
I'll be bail, now, is whiskey and wather.

Oh! long life to the man that invinted potheen –
Sure the Pope ought to make him a marthyr –
If myself was this moment Victoria, our queen,
I'd drink nothing but whiskey and wather!

FROM *WHISKEY AND WATHER* (ANON.)

'Ye may tak a man tae drink, but ye canna mak him water it.'

Captain Martin Becher gave his name to the best-known obstacle in the Aintree Grand National when he fell from his horse, Conrad, into a brook during the 1839 running of the great steeplechase. Becher is reputed to have emerged from the stream and told onlookers how appalling water tasted without the benefit of whisky.

'It's a fine thing a drap watter', said Para Handy, gasping. 'No a worse thing you could drink,' said Hurricane Jack. 'It rots your boots; what'll it no' do to your inside? Watter's fine for sailin' on — there's nothing better — but it's no' drink for sailors.'   NEIL MUNRO, *THE VITAL SPARK* (1906).

'...whisky is now being dashed with lemonade and added to a glass of cider. So long as the 'whisky' is pure patent still, a man is correctly fortifying his lemonade — which possibly needs it — and cider.'   NEIL GUNN.

In Compton Mackenzie's *Rockets Galore* John Farquharson informs his guests that he has '...a rather special bottle of malt...'

'Malt?' Colonel Bullingham, a button-headed man with pale-blue prominent eyes, echoed in surprise.

'Malt whisky.'

'Thanks very much,' said the Colonel. 'I'll try anything once. Fill it up with soda, please.'

'She poured a fat slug of mellow looking Scotch into my glass, and squirted in some fizz-water. It was the sort of liquor you think you can drink forever, and all you do is get reckless'.

RAYMOND CHANDLER, *FAREWELL, MY LOVELY* (1940).

As a boy in Caithness during the years before the First World War, my grandfather often accompanied his father in the family travelling shop, touring crofts and farms from their base in Wick. Many years later he recalled that he had always been curious as to why, when they stopped at one particular farm near Dunbeath, he was given a glass of milk, still warm from the cow, while his father appeared only to get a glass of water. The 'water' was, of course, new spirit from a local illicit still.

When, a few years later, grandfather graduated to village hall dances, he always followed the custom of taking with him a half-bottle of whisky. At harvest-time, each half-bottle was duly secreted in a sheaf of oats or barley in a field near to the dance hall. Between dances there would be a procession of lads – and occasionally lasses – moving between hall and field for refreshment – and occasionally a little more. Usually drink was banned from the halls themselves, and as grandfather and his friends had often travelled from their home village into hostile territory, production of a bottle during the dancing would almost certainly have led to a fight for its possession between 'locals' and 'visitors'.

Frequently, as the evening wore on, a fight along territorial lines took place anyway, with nobody remembering next day just what had been said or done to cause it.

The following is entitled 'A Sup of Good Whiskey' (anon), and appeared in *Lovers' Lyrics of Ireland* (1867). Perhaps it sounds better when accompanied by music and a glass or three...

A sup of good whiskey will make you glad;
Too much of the Creatur' will make you mad;
If you take it in reason, 'twill make you wise;
If you drink to excess, it will close up your eyes:
Yet father and mother,
And sister and brother,
They all take a sup in their turn.

Some preachers will tell you that whiskey is bad;
I think so too – if there's none to be had;
Teetotalers bid you drink none at all;
But, while I can get it, a fig for them all!
Both layman and brother
In spite of this pother,
Will all take a sup in their turn.

Some doctors will tell you 'twill hurt your health;
The justice will say 'twill reduce your wealth;
Physicians and lawyers both do agree,
When your money's all gone, they can get no fee.
Yet surgeon and doctor,
And lawyer and proctor,
Will all take a sup in their turn.

If a soldier is drunk on his duty found,
He to the three-legged horse is bound,
In the face of his regiment obliged to strip;
But a noggin will soften the nine-tailed whip.
For sergeant and drummer,
And likewise His Honour,
Will all take a sup in their turn.

The Turks who arrived from the Porte sublime,
All told us that drinking was held a great crime;
Yet, after their dinner away they slunk,
And tippled, so sly, till they got quite drunk.
For Sultan and Crommet,
And even Mahomet,
They all take a sup in their turn.

The Quakers will bid you from drink abstain,
By yea and by nea they will make it plain;
But some of the broad-brims will get the stuff,
And tipple away till they've tippled enough.
For Stiff-back and Steady,

And Solomon's lady,
Will all take a sup in their turn.

The Germans do say they can drink the most,
The French and Italians also do boast:
Ould Ireland's the country (for all their noise)
For generous drinking and hearty boys.
There each jovial fellow
Will drink till he's mellow,
And take off his glass in his turn.

Inevitably, the most dramatic stories of whisky-drinking are those about occasions when imbibers have gone beyond the 'nine or ten' and have degenerated into drinking...

Samuel Morewood in his 1838 *History of Inebriating Liquors* writes of the 16th century that 'Notwithstanding the frequent use of spirits at that period, our wealthy and luxurious countrymen indulged in the use of rich and costly wines. Hollinshed, in his Chronicles, says that the great Shane O'Neill, who proved so violent an opponent to Elizabeth, usually kept in his cellar at Dundrum, 200 tuns of wine, of which, as well as usquebaugh, he drank copiously, and sometimes to such excess, that his attendants were often obliged to bury him in the earth, chin-deep, until the heating effects of the intoxication had abated'.

There is a story in the *Book of Leinster* about a feast held at Dundabheann, near Bushmills in County Antrim in the north-east corner of Ireland. Some of the guests consumed so much 'inebriating liquor' during the feast that they set off at midnight to travel home to Louth, further down the east coast, but eventually arrived in Kerry in the south-west of the country some days – and some 250 miles off target – later!

'Simon Fraser's entertainment at Castle Downie was famous, as was that of his protagonist and neighbour Forbes, at Culloden House. In both establishments, stretcher-bearers stood by to carry the faint off to their bedrooms.'

JAMES ROSS.

Lord Cockburn recorded in his *Journal of Henry Cockburn* (1874) that at Kilravock Castle in the Highlands there was formerly '...a sort of household officer...whose duty was to prevent the drunk guests from choking'. He recalled Henry Mackenzie, author of *The Man of Feeling*, telling him that he '...was once at a festival there, towards the close of which the exhausted topers sank gradually back and down on their chairs, till little of them was seen above the table except their noses; and at last they disappeared altogether and fell on the floor. Those who were too far gone to rise lay still there from necessity; while those who, like the Man of Feeling, were glad of a pretence for escaping fell into a dose from policy. While Mackenzie was in this state he was alarmed by feeling a hand about his throat, and called out. A voice answered,

"Dinna be feared, Sir; it's me."

"And who are you?"

"A'm the lad that louses the craavats".'

A less indulgent view of Highland drinking habits occurs in Edward Burt's *Letters from a Gentleman in the North of Scotland* (1754).

'Some of the Highland Gentlemen are immoderate Drinkers of Usky, even three or four Quarts at a Sitting; and in general, the People that can pay the Purchase, drink it without Moderation.

'Not long ago, four English Officers took a Fancy to try their Strength in this Bow of Ulysses, against a like Number of the Country Champions, but the Enemy came off victorious; and one of the Officers was thrown into a Fit of the Gout, without Hopes; another had a most dangerous Fever, a third lost his Skin and Hair by Surfeit, and the last confessed to me, that when Drunkenness and Debate run high, he took several Opportunities to sham it.

'They say for Excuse, the Country requires a great deal; but I think they mistake a Habit and Custom for Necessity...those who drink of it to any Degree of Excess behave, for the most Part, like true Barbarians, I think much beyond the Effect of other Liquors.'

Burt's views are at odds with those of the author of the entry in the *Statistical Account of Scotland* (1793) for the parish of Moulin, near Pitlochry, in Perthshire.

'There are two licensed stills of 30 gallons each in the parish, and 24 licensed retailers of ale, beer, and other exciseable liquors. The number of distillers and retailers may be considered as a circumstance unfavourable to the health, and the morals of the people. However, it cannot be said, that the people are addicted to drinking. Even at weddings, and on holidays, instances of persons drinking to excess are few, and a drunken squabble is extremely rare. It is somewhat remarkable, that among people who hardly know how to make a bargain, or pay a debt, except over a dram of whisky, moderation should be so generally observed; particularly when it is considered, that at the fairs, every house, hut, and shed in the respective villages, is converted into a dram-shop.'

Perhaps it was just that the folk of Perthshire could hold their liquor better than most.

During the 1830s people over the age of 15 drank, on average, almost a bottle of whisky per week.

Those younger than 15 were also known to take a dram...

'Sometimes a floater's wife or bairn would come with a message; such a messenger was always offered whisky. Aunt Mary had a story that one day a woman with a child in her arms, and another bit thing at her knee, came up among them; the horn cup was duly handed to her, she took a 'gey guid drap' herself, and then gave a little to each of the babies. "My goodness, child," said my mother to the wee thing that was trotting by its mother's side, "doesn't it bite you?" "Ay, but I like the bite," replied the creature.'

ELIZABETH GRANT OF ROTHIEMURCHUS
MEMOIRS OF A HIGHLAND LADY (1898).

'Now I don't know if you remember the first time you ever tasted whisky and the tremendous shock to the nervous system that is. In Scotland this usually happens around the age of four...'

BILLY CONNOLLY, *GULLIBLE'S TRAVELS* (1982).

The great eighteenth-century Perthshire fiddler and composer Neil Gow was known to partake of a dram to lubricate his bowing arm, and the story is told of how late one night, after playing at a celebration in Perth, Gow unsteadily surveyed the road home to the village of Inver, near Dunkeld, and realised that it was not the length of the road that concerned him, but its breadth.

The lyrics of the song *Neil Gow's Fareweel to Whisky* were written by Agnes Lyon (1762-1840), the wife of Dr Lyon, Minister of Glamis, and were intended to be sung to an air composed by Neil Gow:

> Ye've surely heard o famous Neil,
> The man that played the fiddle weel;
> I wat he was a canty chiel.
> > An' dearly lo'ed the Whisky, O.
> An' aye since he wore tartan hose,
> He dearly lo'ed the Athole Brose;
> An' wae was he, you may suppose,
> To bid fareweel to whisky, O.

Alake, quo' Neil, I'm frail an' auld,

And find my bluid grows unco cauld,

I think it maks me blythe and bauld

      A wee drop Highland whisky, O.

But a' the doctors do agree

      That whisky's no the drink for me;

I'm fleyed they'll gar me tyne my glee,

      Should they part me and whisky, O.

But I should mind on 'auld lang syne',

How paradise our friends did tyne,

Because something ran in their min' –

      Forbid, like Highland whisky, O.

While I can get both wine and ale,

And find my head and fingers hale,

I'll be content, though legs should fail,

      And though forbidden whisky, O.

I'll tak my fiddle in my hand,

And screw the strings up while they stand,

And mak a lamentation grand

      For guid auld Highland whisky, O!

O! a' ye pow'rs o music, come.

I find my heart grows unco glum;

My fiddlestrings will hardly bum

      To say, 'Fareweel to whisky, O'.

fleyed: afraid

tyne: lose

bum: sound

Mackintosh of Borlum, near Fort Augustus, wrote of the 1730s:

    'When I came to a friend's house in the morning I used to be asked if I had my morning draught yet. Now I am asked if I have yet had my tea. And in lieu of the big Quaigh with strong ale and toast, and after a dram of good wholesome Scots spirits, there is now the tea kettle put to the fire, the tea table and silver and china equipage brought in, with marmalet, cream and cold tea'.

    Dr Johnson in *A Journey to the Western Isles of Scotland* (1775) noted 'A man of the Hebrides as soon as he appears in the morning swallows a glass of whisky; yet they are not a drunken race, at least I was never present at much intemperance; but no man is so abstemious as to refuse the morning dram which they call a skalk.'

Edward Dwelly in his *Illustrated Gaelic-English Dictionary* (1901-11) defines 'skalk' as '...a bumper of spirits taken before breakfast...a morning dram', and goes on to itemise a fascinating list of other 'morning drams' usually offered to a (presumably hardy) guest in a house in Gaeldom. First came the sgailc-nide, 'a full bumper of whisky while still lying down', followed by the friochd-uilinn, 'an elbow nip when he was first propped up', after which came the deoch chas-ruisgte, 'when still barefoot', and finally the deoch bhleth, 'while his breakfast porrage oats were being ground'.

'You're not drunk if you can lie on the floor without holding on'.

DEAN MARTIN.

A traveller in the Highlands in 1736 noted, 'The ruddy complexion, nimbleness of these people is not owing to the water drinking but to the aqua vitae, a malt spirit which is commonly used both as victual and drink.' James Ross adds, 'To a certain extent this is the Highland view to this day'.

'Formerly every event was made an occasion for drinking. If it was raining, it was "we'll have a dram to keep out the wet"; if it was cold, "we'll have a dram to keep out the cold; and if it was a fine day, why then "we'll drink its health".'

JA MACCULLOCH, *THE MISTY ISLE OF SKYE* (1905).

Old Scots saying: 'One whisky is alright, two are too much, but three are too few'.

'I tried the all-whisky diet. I lost three days'.

Excessive consumption tends to lead to excessive hangovers.

The traditional Scottish hangover cure is a large measure of the country's other national drink, Irn Bru, while the Japanese allegedly deal with over-indulgence in whisky by eating a pickled cherry next morning.

One cure dating from the Middle Ages involves slicing up an eel and spreading bitter almonds over it before eating it – or being sick, whichever occurs first.

There is even a Haitian voodoo cure, which entails sticking 13 pins into the cork of the bottle you drank from.

'For a bad hangover take the juice of two quarts of whisky.'

EDDIE CONDON.

The American actor and humorist WC Fields was a dedicated imbiber, and he numbered whisky among his (many) favourite drinks. 'A woman drove me to drink and I never even wrote to thank her', he once said.

'Always carry a flagon of whisky in case of a snake bite', he advised his friends. 'And furthermore always carry a small snake'.

Fields' favoured hangover cure was a martini made with one part vermouth to four parts of gin, accompanied by one olive. He was very particular about the olive.

Hangover cures vary from the eminently sensible to the patently ludicrous, and most drinkers have their own favourite methods of dealing with the results of alcoholic excesses, ranging from drinking the classic, cognac-based Prairie Oyster to eating fish fingers or even a fried canary.

Writing in 1694, Robert Boyle advocated the following hangover cure: 'Take green Hemlock that is tender, and put it in your socks, so that it may lie thinly between them and the Soles of your Feet; shift the Herbs once a day'.

Dean Martin's favourite is much less labour-intensive: 'Stay drunk'.

The Norwegian with a hangover says – if he is able – 'jeg har tommermenn', which translates as 'I have carpenters in my head.' For Germans it is 'katzenjammer' – 'a wailing of cats.'

The earliest recorded hangover cure comes from the Greek philosopher Antiphanes. In 479BC he wrote (though in Greek) 'Take the hair, it is well written/of the dog by which you are bitten/work off one wine by his brother/one labour with another'.

Even that great whisky evangelist Neil Gunn was aware of the damage that could be done by drink. Writing of industrial Scotland in the late 19th and early 20th centuries, he notes 'Whisky was the true witch's brew, the real bottled spirit of the Satanic master'.

'...whisky became the national whore and lost her reputation so utterly that to this day even English Chancellors of the Exchequer continue to squeeze the last shilling of her immoral earnings out of her with an exhorbitant shamelessness.'

'Whisky...is drunk for all sorts of illegitimate reasons, as by journalists to quieten conscience, by the timid to avert catarrh, by inferior poets to whip up rhymes, and by commercial travellers to dull the memory of rebuffs.'

AENEAS MACDONALD

The eighteenth-century Gaelic writer and scholar Lachlan MacPherson penned a song which lampooned those who were unable to hold their whisky while drinking in a group. The song extends to 21 verses, and the following is a sample:

> A man of my heart is whisky
> They all wait on him
> He has often felled heroes
> Without unsheathing a sword.

> What else can make us happy
> If women and drink cannot do it?

> You will get the strongest hands there
> And who better than the country lads?
> Even a man at the urine runnel
> Could fell three of them.

> They are full of courage and strength
> Spirited and quick in action;
> Twenty of them at that time
> Would crown red-haired Charlie.

Though Martinmas dues remain unpaid,
Though the King should mount his mother,
They will drink their healing balm
Till their sinews weaken.

As the city of Dundee developed as an industrial centre during the Victorian era, it gained an unenviable reputation for drunkeness and associated high levels of crime and violence. Winston Churchill represented Dundee in parliament from 1908 to 1922, and he called it 'the most drunken city in the British Empire'.

The temperance movement began in Dundee, and the Prohibition Party of Great Britain was founded there. In 1922, Churchill lost the seat to Edwin Scrymgeour, Britain's only Prohibition Party MP.

In the early years of the twentieth century the police in Dundee pioneered a project which circulated photographs, physical descriptions and conviction details of known drunken troublemakers. This can be seen as an extremely early example of the 'Pub-watch' scheme introduced in parts of Scotland almost a century later.

Interestingly, the vast majority of Dundonians prosecuted for drunkenness were women, no doubt due to the largely female workforce of the jute industry on which much of the city's prosperity depended.

'Poet and Tragedian' William McGonagall spent most of his life in Dundee, and was a staunch supporter of the temperance movement:

> Strong drink to the body can do no good;
> It defiles the blood, likewise the food,
> And causes the drunkard with pain to groan,
> Because it extracts the marrow from the bone.
>
> The more's the pity, I must say,
> That so many men and women are by it led astray
> And decoyed from the paths of virtue and led on to vice
> By drinking too much alcohol and acting unwise.

The following is an unequivocally anti-drink piece, translated from the Gaelic singing of Nan MacKinnon of the Isle of Vatersay, and quoted by James Ross. The lyric takes the form of a speech by the 'son of malt', in which he boasts of his powers over men, despite the sometimes doubtful ingedients of which he is made up.

> O do not reject me,
> I am a merry youth,
> Do not be ashamed, my dear,
> To come seeking me,
> And although I have given death
> To your kinsfolk, you know
> That at New Year
> You will carry me in a jar.

I am a noble man
Who subdues millions,
I help to place the rope
Round their necks;
I drown some of them
Without putting a hand to any
And I make their kinsfolk
Weep and blubber.

And the smith in the smithy
Would pawn his anvil
To find the place
From where I come,
And the wright
His claw hammer to seek me,
And the mason his trowel
Though he would bewail it later.

And the weaver and the clerk
Doughty men,
They leapt at each other
Their shirts in ribbons,
Such blood in their noses
Gladdened my heart,
Their feet through their shoes
Their buttocks through their breeks.

If you understood my nature
You would not give a penny for me;
I am made of soap and mud;
If you understood my nature
You would never buy me,
I have a little of the 'blue stone'
Many a thing it contains.

O do not reject me
I am a merry youth;
Do not be ashamed, my dear,
To come seeking me,
And although I have given death
To your kinsfolk, you know
That at New Year
You will carry me in a jar.

'We have a story of a young man that was long tempted by the devil to commit one of three sins: either to kill his father, ravish his mother, or be drunk, he chose the last as most innocent; but when drunk committed both the other.'

RICHARD LAWRENCE
*THE INTEREST OF IRELAND
IN ITS TRADE AND WEALTH STATED* (1682).

It is recorded that during the 1830s the cities of Glasgow and Edinburgh boasted one public house for every 130 residents. Twenty years later legislation was introduced to curb the extent of drinking in Scotland, and particularly drinking in public. In Glasgow the only legal outlets for alcohol on a Sunday became the numerous pleasure boats which plied their trade 'doon the watter'. The availability of alcohol on board added to the allure of a day trip to Rothesay for many passengers, and the essentially Glaswegian metaphor for being drunk – 'steaming' – has its origins in those Clyde excursions.

During the 1960s a Scottish folk group was booked to play at a large country house in the Borders. In the course of the evening the group's members became somewhat drink-taken, and finally went off to their attic bedroom with a couple of bottles of whisky, which were duly consumed. It soon became obvious that the room was too hot for anyone to sleep in, so one member of the group decided to open a window. Unfortunately, he was far too inebriated to accomplish this task, and decided instead to throw his boot in the general direction of the window. There was a smashing of glass, and a few minutes later everyone agreed that the fresh breeze was very welcome. They soon fell asleep. In daylight it transpired that the musician had thrown his boot at a mirror.

There are many intriguing tales concerning whisky and the church, in some of which the clergy takes a disapproving stance on drinking, while in others...

The Rev. John Grant wrote in 1790 of Tomintoul, the highest

village in the Highlands, situated not far from Glenlivet, 'Tammtoul...is inhabited by thirty seven families, without a single manufacture...All of them sell whisky and all of them drink it. When disengaged from this business the women spin yarn, kiss their inamoratos, or dance to the discordant sounds of an old fiddle'.

Despite the apparent attractions of such a lifestyle, we must assume that the Reverend Grant disapproved.

A minister returned to his parish from a meeting of the General Assembly in Edinburgh. A few days later he was stopped in the street by one of his parishioners who pointed out that he had just come from the railway station, where there was a wooden box addressed to the minister.

'Oh, that's just some books I bought while I was in Edinburgh', he explained.

'Weel, I'd no' leave them there for lang', replied the parishioner, 'When I saw them, you're books were leakin''.

James Ross cites the example of a newly-ordained minister in Kintail, a Mr Chisholm, who in 1720 complained that Murdo MacRae and some fellow clansmen had broken into his manse, where they had caused damage and then chased the naked minister from his bedroom, firing at him as he left. The complaint concludes that MacRae and his compatriots '...did plunder and carry off thirty gallons of whisky from the manse'. Unfortunately, no explanation is given for why a manse should have been so liberally supplied with whisky in the first place.

Ross also notes that the Reverend Archibald Campbell of Morvern was accused in 1733 of being drunk at a baptism. In his defence he stated that he was merely in a state of what would be called in Gaelic corra-ghleus. This, he said, was 'no more than that cheerful humour which a moderate glass puts into one'.

A minister was rumoured to be too fond of whisky for the good of his position. When a kirk elder was asked by the Bishop if he had ever seen the minister the worse for drink he replied 'I canna say I've seen him the waur o'drink, but nae doubt I've seen him the better o't'.

In January 1999 Sutherland crofter Hector Stewart was buried in a plot on his own land with no minister present. Instead, a case of whisky occupied the position where the minister would usually have stood, and Hector's family and friends toasted him in the whisky. He had specified that he wished to be buried on his own croft, while surrounded by his friends drinking whisky.

The Presbytery was meeting in a Highland town one market day, and a minister spotted a farmer who was a member of his flock heading for the door of a nearby pub. Wishing to ask him about his nonattendence at kirk on a number of Sundays, the minister shouted to the farmer, who ignored him and carried on towards the pub. In an effort to get the man's attention, the minister even whistled. There was no response from the farmer.

Determined to rebuke the farmer, the minister waited for quite a while until the suitably refreshed farmer emerged from the pub. 'Did you not hear me calling to you, and even whistling?' asked the irritated minister.

'Oh, I heerd ye a'richt', he replied, 'but I hed only the price o' the wan wee dram.'

'Is there anything more to be put ashore, Donald?' queried the captain of a steamer at a pier in the West Highlands. 'Aye, sir' answered Donald, 'There's the twa-gallon jar o'whisky for the Established meenister.' 'For the Established minister, Donald?' said the captain, laughing. 'Are ye quite sure it's no for the Free Kirk minister?' 'Quite, sir,' said Donald cannily. 'The Free Kirk meenister aye gets his whisky-jar sent in the middle o' a barrel o' flour!' WILLIAM HARVEY, *SCOTTISH LIFE & CHARACTER* (1899).

Alec the barber was suffering from a serious hangover, and while trimming the minister's hair he inadvertently nicked his ear. 'It's a terrible affliction, the whisky', said the minister reprovingly. 'Aye', replied Alec. 'It mak's the skin awfy tender'.

Those whisky drinkers seeking medical approval for their indulgence may delve back into history and point out that in 1505 the Guild of Barber Surgeons of Edinburgh was granted a monopoly on the manufacture of whisky in the Scottish capital. Need we say more.

We may also seize on recent medical pronouncements that confirm what all right-thinking people have always known – taken in moderation, whisky can be beneficial to one's health.

And then we have Holinshed, even if we don't understand much of what he is saying...

Probably the most extravagant claims for the powers of whisky were made by Raphael Holinshed in his *The History of Ireland* (1577). Holinshed was referring to a treatise by Theoricus on Aqua vitae when he wrote '...It dryeth up the breakying out of handes, and killeth the fleshe wormes, if you wash your handes therewith. It skourethe all skurfe and skaldes from the head, beyng therewith daily washte before meales. Beyng moderately taken, sayth he, it soeth age, it strengtheneth youth, it helpeth digestion, it cutteth fleume, it abandoneth melancholy, it relisheth the hart, it lighteneth the mynd, it quickeneth the spirites, it cureth the hydropsie, it healeth the strangury, it ounceth the stone, it expelleth grauell, it puffeth away all Ventositie, it kepeth and preserueth the hed from whirlyng, the eyes from dazelyng, the tongue from lispying, the mouth from mafflyng, the teeth from chatteryng, the throte from ratling, the weasan from stieflyng, wirtchyng, the guts from rumblyng, the handes from shiuering, the sinowes from shrinkyng, the veynes from crumpling, the bones from akying, the marrow from soakying...And truly, it is a soueraigne liquor, if it be orderlie taken.'

From *The White Horse Bulletin* for Christmas 1934.

'A Scot rushed into a railway carriage in an excited state, shouting: "Whisky, quick – has anybody got a flask, a woman's just fainted in the corridor."

An old gentleman produced a flask and handed it to the Scot. The Scot unscrewed the cap and took a large draught, and handed it back to the owner, saying: "That's better. It always upsets me to see a woman faint." '

It seems from that same *White Horse Bulletin* that in those days good doctors could still be relied upon to prescribe a drop of the cratur as a tonic. And they say medicine has advanced...

'A doctor ordered the old vicar to take some hot whisky each day. "But," objected the patient, "I'm afraid my housekeeper would leave me if I did."

"She need not know," replied the doctor. Just tell her you want some shaving water."

Some weeks later the doctor called at the house to inquire for the vicar.

"He's gone quite mad, sir," quavered the housekeeper. "The poor unfortunate gentleman's shaving himself morning, noon and night." '

and...

' "Has your husband taken the medicine I prescribed? A tablet before each meal and a small WHITE HORSE after?"

"Mebbe he's a few tablets behind, but he's a month ahead wi' th' whisky." '

Away your pills, it'll cure all ills,

Be ye Pagan, Christian or Jew.

So take off your coat and grease your throat

With a bucketful of mountain dew.

THE RARE OULD MOUNTAIN DEW (TRAD.).

An apparently effective cure for diarrhoea – along with the advice not to cough too much – is to drink a measure of whisky which has first been ignited by a match. Remember, of course, to extinguish the flames before consumption.

Evan Williams built the first commercial distillery in Kentucky in the 1780s, and he distilled from corn. More than a century later it was recorded that Williams' spirit was '...a good medicine for chills and fever, though a very bad whisky'.

Old Scottish cold remedy: Retire to bed with a large whisky toddy. Hang a bowler hat at the foot of the bed. Drink until there appear to be two hats.

'I remember the first bottle of Early Times bourbon I ever bought. My experience with whisky at that time was limited to its medicinal use in colds,

flu, muscular aches and pains, constipation, diarrhea, pin worms and piles. Once I used it for jockey strap itch, and discovered if taken internally the effect was more lasting and much more palatable. This was during Prohibition, when you needed a doctor's prescription to get drunk.'

HARRY HARRISON KROLL.

In 1983 the Conservative peer Lord Boothby was openly critical of the high level of taxation that his government levied on Scotch whisky, querying whether 'Her Majesty's Government realise that in the modern world Scotch whisky is about the only thing left that brings guaranteed and sustained comfort to mankind.'

Boothby received support from the unlikely source of veteran socialist Lord Shinwell, at the time in his hundredth year. 'Manny' Shinwell tried to have whisky prescribed on the National Health, and when that was unsuccessful he moved, tongue-in-cheek, that it should at least be deemed tax-deductible for members of the House of Lords on the grounds that '…there is general consumption of this liquid by noble Lords, and since many of them cannot do without it because it is in the nature of a medicine'.

The horse and mule live thirty years
And nothing know of wines and beers.
The goat and sheep at twenty die
And never taste a scotch or rye.
The cow drinks water by the ton
And at eighteen is mostly done.

The dog at fifteen cashes in

Without the aid of rum and gin.

The cat in milk and water soaks

And then in twelve short years it croaks.

The modest, sober, bone-dry hen

Lays eggs for nogs and dies at ten.

All animals are strictly dry

But sinful, ginful, beer-soaked men

survive for three-score years and ten,

While some of them, a very few,

Stay pickled till they're ninety-two.

ANON.

'To me was known MacLeod's custom, broaching wine, drinking beer and filling the stoup with the thrice-distilled stuff, the necessary spur to promote enjoyment.' MARY MACLEOD, SEVENTEENTH CENTURY SKYE BARD.

Mary lived to the age of 105, dying in 1705, reputedly her last words being translated as 'Ho ro, how I enjoy the dram! Many a person is indebted to it'.

Another Gaelic bard, Duncan Ban Macintyre from Glenorchy also wrote in praise of whisky. He served as a soldier in the Edinburgh Town Guard and was once charged with making and selling illicit whisky. His wife Mary was a noted distiller, who reputedly kept a still concealed beneath the howff she ran on the city's Royal Mile. Duncan declared to the magistrates that he had drunk far more whisky in his life than he had ever made, and the charge was dismissed! It seems likely that some – if not all – of the assembled magistrates had been customers of the Mackintyre family still...

> The elegant stuff will cause us to sing in melody.
> Its joy will make our conversation more eloquent.
> This is the true sweet drink which assuages our thirst.
> Sad would it be if it were taken from us.
> A health to the heroes, the splendid Highlanders,
> Whose custom it was to drink down their dram!
> They were ever lovers of the tasty stuff.
>
> DUNCAN BAN MACINTYRE, *'SONG OF THE BOTTLE'*.

The 'tasty stuff' clearly didn't shorten Macintyre's life. Though he couldn't quite match Mary MacLeod, he did live to the age of 88, which was quite a feat in the eighteenth century. He died in Edinburgh in 1812.

On Monday 8th November 1999 Eva Morris of Stone in Staffordshire added a measure of whisky to her afternoon cup of tea. Nothing remarkable in that, perhaps, except that it was Eva's 114 birthday, and she was believed to be the oldest person in Britain. It had long been her habit to lace her tea with whisky, and as Richard Britten, director of the nursing home where Eva lived, remarked, 'At 114 I suppose she's a pretty good advert for the whisky industry'.

'Gie me the real Glenlivet, and I weel believe I could mak' drinking toddy oot o' sea water. The human mind never tires o' Glenlivet, ony mair than o' caller

air. If a body could find oot the exac' proper proportion and quantity that ought to be drunk every day, and keep to that, I verily trow that he might leeve for ever, without dying at a', and that doctors and kirkyards would go oot o' fashion.'

JAMES HOGG, 'THE ETTRICK SHEPHERD'.

According to David Milsted in *Bluff Your Way In Whisky*, two things are certain about whisky:

    1. No two whiskies are alike.

    2. 99 per cent of whisky drinkers can't tell the difference until it's revealed to them. Keep pointing out number (1) while bearing number (2) in mind, and you can't go wrong.

'...their plenty of corn was such as disposed the natives to brew several sorts of liquor, as common usquebaugh, another called trestarig, id est, aqua-vitae, three times distilled, which is strong and hot; a third sort is four times distilled, and this by the natives is called usquebaugh-baul, id est usquebaugh, which at first taste affects all the members of the body: two spoonfuls of this last liquor is a sufficient dose; and if any man exceed this, it would presently stop his breath, and endanger his life'.

MARTIN MARTIN, A DESCRIPTION OF THE WESTERN HIGHLANDS, (1703).

Friend, by my soul, I'll whiskey drink,

'Tis better far than beer:

'Tis not so heavy I do think,

Although it is more dear:

Like to fair woman's blush,

That steals away your heart,

It quickly drowns your brains in lush,

With senses do depart.

Come, take a drop with my, my blade,

We'll get drunk, and soon,

And when we on the floor are laid,

We'll snore away till noon.

Perhaps you think it is not paid,

But that I chalk a score –

Of that, my boy, be not afraid,

But drink and call for more.

ANON, FROM *'THE DUBLIN COMIC SONGSTER'* (1853).

In August 1822 King George IV visited Edinburgh, a momentous occasion which was largely stage-managed by Sir Walter Scott. The corpulent monarch chose to wear an excessively long kilt for the visit, accompanied by a pair of white tights. This must have detracted somewhat from the carefully contrived Brigadoon version of Scottish life which Sir Walter presented to his majesty...

JG Lockhart in his *The Life of Sir Walter Scott* (1848) describes the king's arrival at Leith. '...on receiving the poet on the quarter-deck, his Majesty called for a bottle of Highland whisky, and having drunk his health in this national liquor, desired a glass to be filled for him. Sir Walter, after draining his own bumper, made a request that the King would condescend to bestow on him the glass out of which his Majesty had just drunk his health; and this being granted, the precious vessel was immediately wrapped up and carefully deposited in what he conceived to be the safest part of his dress.'

When he returned home, Scott found that the poet George Crabbe had arrived on a visit. 'The royal gift was forgotten – the ample skirt of the coat within which it had been packed, and which he had hitherto held cautiously in front of his person, slipped back to its more usual position – he sat down beside Crabbe, and the glass was crushed to atoms. His scream and gesture made his wife conclude that he had sat down on a pair of scissors' or the like; but very little harm had been done except the breaking of the glass, of which alone he had been thinking'.

Also relating to King George's Scottish visit:

Lord Conyngham, the Chamberlain, was looking everywhere for pure Glenlivet whisky: the king drank nothing else. It was not to be had out of the Highlands. My father sent word to me – I was the cellarer – to empty my pet bin, where was whisky long in wood, long in uncorked bottles, mild as milk, and the true contraband gout in it. Much as I grudged this treasure it made our fortunes afterwards, showing on what trifles great events depend. The whisky, and fifty brace of ptarmigan, all shot by one man, went up to Holyrood House, and were graciously received and made much of, and a reminder of this attention at a proper moment by the gentlemanly Chamberlain ensured to my father the Indian Judgeship.

ELIZABETH GRANT OF ROTHIEMURCHUS,
MEMOIRS OF A HIGHLAND LADY (1898).

Tom Morton (*Spirit of Adventure*) writes about the malt whisky 'As We Get It', which is bottled by JG Thomson. It is a vatting of several malts, most notably The Macallan, and is bottled at cask strength.

'Getting drunk on this stuff is like being assaulted with an empty sherry cask, then being left for dead upside down inside it with an open tin of Evo-Stik beside you.'

'Here lies one who might be trusted with untold gold, but not with unmeasured whisky.'   SIR WALTER SCOTT'S EPITAPH FOR HIS
FAVOURITE SERVANT, TOM PURDIE.

A highly successful advertising campaign for The Macallan single malt whisky which ran during the 1980s featured humorous anecdotes, submitted by aficionados of the Speyside classic.

One such story came from Commander Peter Craig, who wrote:

'As a wee lad, I once accompanied Grandfather, his ghillie, and Ben, the Labrador, to fish for salmon; but disaster struck and I fell into the Spey's icy swirling waters.

'Ben leapt in to retrieve me and near death, I and the exhausted dog were hauled to the bank.

' "Quick, Hamish! The Macallan!" cried Grandfather.

'A large dram was poured down Ben's throat and, in a trice, he was on his feet, licking colour back into my frozen cheeks.

'"A near thing!" gasped Grandfather.

'"Aye, replied Hamish, "Ah dinna ken where we'd ha' found anither dog like Ben".'

An Englishman and an Irishman were fishing together. Both were using worms, but while the Englishman was catching nothing, the Irishman was doing very well. Before attaching each worm to his hook, the Irishman dipped it in a bottle of Irish whiskey at his side. 'Do the fish like the whiskey?' asked the Englishman. 'No', replied his fellow angler, 'with a drop of whiskey inside him the worm just ups and grabs hold of the fish and pulls him out by the throat.'

'Do not, unless in an emergency, use paper, plastic or metal. Some cask-strength malts will eat straight through plastic.'
TOM MORTON'S ADVICE ON WHISKY-DRINKING VESSELS.

John Francis Campbell of Islay was an enthusiastic Victorian collector of folk-tales, ably, if sometimes unsteadily, assisted by Hector MacLean. A photograph exists of Campbell, MacLean and Lachlan MacNeil, sitting at a table with a bottle of whisky in the centre. Campbell's diary contains the following delightful entry for 17th August 1870:

'Went from Glasgow to Paisley, and to No.5 Maxwellton Street to Lachlan MacNeil, shoemaker; found him and Hector installed in a small public, both rather screwed, Hector the worse. They have been at the tale of O'Kane's leg for about a week, and Hector has made about 62 sheets of Gaelic x 4 = 248, say about 260 pages of foolscap.'

'First an' foremist don't take any, an' then ye'll nivver hev' it on yer breath. But if ye hev' tuck a sup, or been on the batther for two or three days, go an' stan furnenst a wall that's newly white-washed an' blow yer breath on it for two or three minutes. If that disin't do, go into the garden an' ate a fistful o' parsley; an' if that disin't do still, buy an ounce o' good black tay, an' ate it jist out o' the paper.'

HOW TO AVOID SMELLING OF WHISKEY,
FROM *POOR RABBIN'S OLLMINICK* (1861).

Sir Anthony Acland, British ambassador to the USA, made a speech in Washington to the United States Keepers of the Quaich society in the early 1990s during which he made the point that 'Americans create a pile of empty Scotch whisky bottles as tall as the Empire State Building every three minutes.'

At that time, it was claimed that a bottle of Scotch whisky was drunk every tenth of a second in the USA. Presumably not always by the same person.

Legendary frontiersman Davy Crockett is reputed to have drank a large draught of moonshine in a single gulp on one occasion. When the power of speech returned to him he is said to have commented that it had been so hot he wouldn't need to have his food cooked for a month.

A DISAPPOINTING HOST. – *Sandy*: 'A'm tellt ye hev a new nebbur, Donal'.' *Donald*: 'Aye.' *Sandy*: 'An' what like is he?' *Donald*: 'Weel, he's a curious laddie. A went to hev a bit talk wi' him th' ither evenin', an' he offered me a glass o' whuskey, d'ye see? Weel, he was poorin' it oot, an' A said to him "Stop!" – an' he stoppit! That's the soort o' mon he is.'

Irish drinker to new neighbour who is in the process of pouring him an extremely modest glass of whiskey: 'Sure, it's a fine, steady hand you're having.'

'There is good whisky, there is whisky which is not so good, but there is no bad whisky.'   DR PHILIP SCHIDROWITZ.

'In the worst time a moonlighter slept for a fortnight close to the house of an Irish landlord, who was well aware that he was there for the express purpose of shooting him, but he never even attempted it.

    ' "Time after time I lay in a ditch to have a go at him, but he would ride by, looking for all the world as if he would shoot a flea off the tail of a snipe, so that, with all the whiskey in the world to help me, I dared not do it," was his explanation before he left for America.

'Did you never hear the parish priest's sermon?

' "It's whiskey makes you bate your wives; it's whiskey makes your homes desolate; it's whiskey makes you shoot your landlords and" – with emphasis as he thumped the pulpit – "it's whiskey makes you miss them".'

SAMUEL M HUSSEY, *REMINISCENCES OF AN IRISH LAND AGENT* (1904).

A Martini drinker of my acquaintance is of the opinion that, 'A Martini is like a woman's breasts: One is too few and three is too many.'

Martini and whisky come together in the Smoky Martini cocktail, which consists of three parts gin to one part Islay single malt, shaken over ice and served in a Martini glass.

A whisky cocktail reputedly favoured in the Crown Hotel in Stornoway on the Isle of Lewis is called 'Jelly Beans.' It consists of whisky, vodka, gin, Pernod, cherry brandy, Babycham and lemonade.

Perhaps the most relaxing whisky-based drink of them all is the Brompton Cocktail. Mix whisky, honey, cocaine and morphine. (Author's note: Don't try this one at home.)

Two American Civil War quotes, the first from the leader of the Confederate army, and the second about the Unionist general and subsequent US President, Ulysses S Grant:

'I like it: I always did, and that is the reason I never use it.'
ROBERT E LEE, C.1850.

'Let me know what brand of whiskey Grant uses. For if it makes fighting generals like Grant, I should like to get some of it for distribution.'
ABRAHAM LINCOLN, US PRESIDENT AND POLITICAL
LEADER OF THE NORTHERN STATES.

The first President of the United States, George Washington, was a noted Virginian rye whiskey distiller, and as an army general he advocated the supply of spirits to the troops in order to combat bad weather and fatigue. He noted 'The benefits arising from the moderate use of strong liquor have been experienced in all armies and are not to be disputed.'

Although he should perhaps have known better, Washington precipitated a 'Whiskey Rebellion' in 1792 when he imposed harsh new excise legislation in an attempt to help pay off the national debt which remained from the war of independence.

What was believed to be Washington's own still, bearing the legend 'Made in Bristol, England, 1783', was captured by revenue officers in 1939. They discovered it during a raid on an illicit whiskey-making operation at the home of a black family who were direct descendants of some of Washington's slaves at his Mount Vernon estate.

'No man is genuinely happy, married, who has to drink worse whiskey than he used to drink when he was single.'
HL MENCKEN.

A signalbox on the long-gone Rothes to Keith railway line on Speyside reputedly contained a fire bucket filled with whisky which had been obtained in a questionable manner. The whisky was hidden beneath a layer of sawdust, which gave the appearance of a normally-functioning fire bucket. Any visitors fancying a dram just pushed the sawdust to one side, and dunked a glass.

God and the Archangel Gabriel were discussing the newly-created world. God mentioned that he had made a beautiful country called Scotland, where rivers ran cold and clear and were full of salmon and trout. There were magnificent mountains, lochs and glens, the finest natural foods, and best of all, the secret of how to make the most wonderful drink in the world, uisge beatha, the water of life. Gabriel was duly impressed.

'It seems that you have been very generous to the Scots, oh Creator', he said.

'Not really', replied God. 'I haven't told them who their neighbours are going to be yet.'

Their chiefest drink is milk,
for want of milk, the broth,
They take which thing the surgeon swears
is physic by his troth.
And if that broth be scant
yet water is at hand,

For every river yields enough
within that goodly land.
Again if fortune fawneth
or on them chance to smile,
She fills them with usquebaugh
and wine another while.
O that it cheers in bowls
it beautifieth the feast,
And makes them look with drunken nolls
from most unto the least.
Now when their guts be full
then comes the pastime in,
The bard and harper melody
unto them do begin.

JOHN DERRICKE,
THE IMAGE OF IRELANDE, (1581).

Two men were sitting at a bar, each having the latest in a long series of drams, when they struck up a conversation.

'Where are you from?' asked the first.

'Mull', replied the second.

'Well, well, I'm a Tobermory man myself.'

'Me too.'

'What street in Tobermory?'

At that point the landlord came in to ask the barman how things were going.

'Ach, fine,' he replied, 'except the MacLean twins are pissed again.'

'Buddhists manage celibacy because they don't have whisky.'

BILLY CONNOLLY.

Connoisseurs may wish to know that there is now a whisky-flavoured condom on the market, and not just whisky-flavoured. The 'McCondom' is malt whisky-flavoured.

Imagine the scene. A couple of whisky-lovers are enjoying themselves in the privacy of their own boudoir when suddenly the bedside lamp is switched on. 'Just what sort of girl do you think I am?', asks the female. 'I thought you really cared about me. This is only blended.'

A visitor to Glasgow saw a sign outside a bar which read, 'A pie, a nip and a friendly word: £1.' He went inside, paid his pound and duly consumed the pie and the dram. As he left he asked the barman, 'What's the friendly word?' The barman replied, 'Don't eat the pie.'

A visitor to Ireland (not necessarily the same visitor) saw a sign pointing down a side road which read, *O'Toole's Bar 2 miles*. He was tired and thirsty, so he set off to walk to the bar. Eventually he arrived there in a state of near exhaustion, and ordered a restorative Power's. 'The sign says two miles,' said the visitor, 'but it seemed like a lot further.' 'Well,' said the landlord, 'if it said six miles nobody would come.'

Temperance worker (paying a surprise visit to the home of his pet convert):
'Does Mr MacMurdoch live here?'
Mrs MacMurdoch: 'Aye, carry him in!'.

Chapter 3

Banning it

As the Glaswegian writer Jack House noted, according to the law of Scotland '...you are not allowed to make water in public or whisky in private.'

It is almost certain that on the day in 1644 when the Scottish Parliament imposed the first excise duty on whisky someone decided to make the spirit outwith the law and evade the tax. People have been evading it ever since.

In Ireland they made, and continue to make, poitin, while North and South Carolina, Georgia, Kentucky and Tennessee are the US states most usually associated with 'moonshine.'

Just as the Devil is supposed to have all the best tunes, so the illicit whisky-makers tend to have the best stories...

'Taxation in the UK is extremely high, accounting for as much as 70% of the retail price of a typical bottle of standard blended Scotch whisky.'
SCOTCH WHISKY ASSOCIATION'S *SCOTCH WHISKY: QUESTIONS AND ANSWERS.*

'A hateful tax levied upon commodities, and judged not by the common judges of property, but by wretches hired by those to whom Excise is paid.'
SAMUEL JOHNSON'S *DICTIONARY* DEFINITION OF 'EXCISE' (1755).

The music hall entertainer Will Fyffe sang a popular song with lyrics by David Mackenzie which went:

> It's really high time that something was done
> To alter the way the country is run.
> They're not doing things in the way that they should.
> Och! Just take for instance the price of food.
> It's twelve and tanner a bottle,
> That's what they're asking today.
> It's twelve and tanner a bottle,
> It takes all the pleasure away.
> Before you can get a wee drappie
> You have to spend all that you've got,
> Och! how can a fellow be happy
> When happiness costs such a lot.

'The degradation, recklessness, and destitution which, as a rule, follow in the wake of illicit distillation are notorious to all. I know of three brothers on the West coast. Two of them settled down on crofts, became respectable members of the community, and with care and thrift and hard work even acquired some little means. The third took to smuggling, and has never done anything else; has been several times in prison, has latterly lost all his smuggling utensils, and is now an old broken-down man, without a farthing, without sympathy, without friends, one of the most wretched objects in the whole parish.'

'I know most of the smugglers in my own district personally. With a few exceptions they are the poorest among the people. How can they be otherwise? Their's is the work of darkness, and they must sleep through the day. Their crofts are not half tilled or manured; their houses are never repaired; their very children are neglected, dirty, and ragged. They cannot bear the strain of regular steady work even if they feel disposed. Their moral and physical stamina have become impaired, and they can do nothing except under the unhealthy influence of excitement and stimulants. Gradually their manhood becomes undermined, their sense of honour becomes deadened, and they become violent law-breakers and shameless cheats.'

FORMER EXCISE OFFICER IAN MACDONALD,
SMUGGLING IN THE HIGHLANDS (1914).

Although remote rural areas were obviously safest for illicit distillers – or smugglers as they were known – there were also many instances of urban stills.

In Edinburgh in 1777 there were apparently eight licensed stills, but some 400 unlicensed ones. An illicit whisky-making operation took place during the mid-nineteenth century in the cellars of the Tron Kirk, and another was located in one of the arches below South Bridge. It had been working for 18 months when it was discovered in 1815. A water supply came from tapping into a water mains which ran directly above the still, and the smoke was spirited away via a hole bored into the chimney of the neighbouring house.

Perhaps the cheekiest example of illicit distilling occured in the 'whisky capital' of Dufftown on Speyside. Here an illicit still was set up in the clock tower in the centre of the town square, and the local excise officers passed by it every day. If they ever got a whiff of whisky-making they would naturally have assumed it came from one of the town's numerous legal distilleries. The still is said to have been discovered when one of the excisemen who was an amateur clock repairer noticed that the clock in the tower had stopped, and bounded eagerly up the staircase to examine the mechanism. He was greeted by the sight of a small still, going full tilt.

'Time would fail to tell how spirits, not bodies, have been carried past officers in coffins and hearses, and even in bee-hives. How bothies have been built underground, and the smoke sent up the house lum, or how an ordinary pot has been placed in the orifice of an underground bothy, so as to make it appear that the fire and smoke were aye for washing purposes. At the Falls of Orrin the bothy smoke was made to blend judiciously with the spray of the falls so as to escape notice.'

IAN MACDONALD, SMUGGLING IN THE HIGHLANDS (1914).

An old man who ran the boat-house at Perth harbour bought illicit whisky from ships that berthed there. He had a large garden, and would bury his casks of whisky in the garden, growing vegetables over them. It was often observed during the 'smuggling season' that the vegetables frequently looked to be newly-planted.

Illicit distilling may seem to be a macho, swashbuckling affair, but women played a significant part in it.

One woman from Abriachan was apprehended by a customs officer as she approached Inverness with a jar of illicit whisky. She convinced the exciseman that she was about to faint, and begged for a sip from the jar. This he duly granted, at which point the woman spat the mouthful of whisky into his eyes, and escaped – with the jar- before he could recover his sight.

Vessels filled with illicit spirit were frequently strapped to the stomachs of young women to give the appearance of pregnancy, and one Irish smuggler reputedly had a tin vessel made in the shape of a woman. Filled with poitin and dressed in voluminous clothes and a bonnet, his 'wife' was strapped behind him on his horse, and passed the scrutiny of many an unsuspecting gauger.

'Balfron was a lawless village. It was illicit distillation that demoralised the district. The men of the place resorted to the woods or to the sequestered glens among the Campsie Hills and there distilled whisky, which their wives and daughters took in tin vessels in the form of stays buckled round their waists to sell for a high price in Glasgow.'

MRS ELIZA FLETCHER (1770-1858).

'Various were the ways of "doing" the unpopular gaugers. A cask of spirits was once seized and conveyed by the officers to a neighbouring inn. For safety they took the cask with them into the room they occupied on the second floor. The smugglers came to the inn, and requested the maid who was attending upon the officers to note where the cask was standing. The girl took her bearings so accurately that, by boring through the flooring and bottom of the cask, the spirits were quickly transferred to a suitable vessel placed underneath, and the officers were left guarding the empty cask. An augur hole was shown to me some years ago in the flooring at the Bogroy Inn, where the feat was said to have been performed, but I find that the story is also claimed for Mull. Numerous clever stories are claimed for several localities.'

IAN MACDONALD, *SMUGGLING IN THE HIGHLANDS* (1914).

In a slightly naive early 19th century attempt to curb illicit distilling, a 'reward' of £5 was offered by the government for every worm that was surrendered. As the worm was the most expensive part of the distilling apparatus it became good business for smugglers to turn in worn-out worms and purchase replacements with the reward money.

One Robbie MacPherson of Glenrinnes, near Dufftown, went

a stage further, actually constructing a 'dummy' distilling bothy in which the old still was set up. The gaugers subsequently seized the equipment after being informed of its presence by a member of Robbie's gang, who duly pocketed his £5.

A number of factors conspire to make illicit whisky much harsher than legally distilled spirit. They include a lack of maturation, running the spirit through just one still, and the fact that lack of head-elevation means that all the impurities, all the 'essential oils and acids' as MacDonald calls them, 'pass over with the alcohol into the worm, however carefully distillation is carried out.' 'The smuggler's still has no head elevation', writes MacDonald, 'the still-head being as flat as an old blue bonnet...'

The presence of fusel oils – or heavier alcohols – can cause catastrophic hangovers in the unwary, though some drinkers seem to feel that the fusel oils give their dram character. According to the *Scottish National Dictionary* there was a particularly coarse whisky which once found favour with the carriers of Gilmerton, near Edinburgh. The dictionary gives the following quote by way of illustration: 'He preferred his whisky to be strong and heady, with a suspicion of what he called "Fussle-ile" in it – the variety of potation that is usually called "Kill the Cairter".'

The powers that be were not always as diligent in suppressing the illicit whisky trade as they might have been.

Sir Osgood Mackenzie of Inverewe, in the Western Highlands, wrote in his memoirs *A Hundred Years in the Highlands* (1921) 'My father never tasted any but smuggled whisky, and when every mortal that called for him – they were legion daily – had a dram instantly poured for him, the ankers of whisky emptied yearly must have been numerous indeed. I don't believe my mother or he ever dreamed that smuggling was a crime.'

Osgood Mackenzie became a Justice of the Peace at Fortrose, in Ross-shire, and decided he must stop drinking 'mountain dew', as it was a practice incompatible with sentencing whisky smugglers. 'So ended all my connection with smuggling except in my capacity as magistrate, to the grief of at least one of my old friends and visitors, the Dean of Ross and Argyll, who scoffed at my resolution and looked sorrowfully back on the happy times when he was young and his father distilled every Saturday what was needed for the following week. He was of the same mind as a grocer in Church Street, Inverness, who, though licensed to sell only what was drunk off the premises, notoriously supplied customers in the back shop. Our Pastor, Donald Fraser, censuring this breach of the law, was told "But I never approved of that law!" He and the Dean agreed entirely that the law was iniquitous and should be broken.'

'There can be no doubt that "good, pious" men engaged in smuggling, and there is less doubt that equally good, pious men – ministers and priests – were grateful recipients of a large share of the smuggler's produce.

'Some of the old lairds not only winked at the practice, but actually encouraged it. Within the last thirty years, if not twenty years, a tenant on the

Brahan estate had his rent account credited with the price of an anchor of smuggled whisky, and there can be no doubt that rents were frequently paid directly and indirectly by the produce of smuggling.'

IAN MACDONALD, *SMUGGLING IN THE HIGHLANDS* (1914).

In *A Highland Parish, or the History of Fortingall* (1928), Alexander Stewart noted that breaches of the game and excise laws '...were not regarded as in any sense immoral, and were regularly committed by people who in all other respects were law-abiding citizens of the most irreproachable character. Not only so, but even magistrates who tried such cases often refused to take a serious view of them. At the beginning of the nineteenth century such offences were tried by the courts of the Justices of the Peace. At Weem [near Aberfeldy], where the local court met, there was often a long list of smuggling and poaching cases before the magistrates; but Francis Mor, the chief of the Macnabs, who usually presided, as a general rule, let the delinquents off lightly.'

On one occasion The Macnab is even reputed to have provided a smuggler with a key which gave him access to where a cask of whisky which had been confiscated from him was being held as evidence in a forthcoming court case. The cask was duly swapped with one of water, and Macnab, in his role of JP, dismissed the case in mock fury after having the contents of the cask tested in court, charging the luckless exciseman involved with contempt of court into the bargain!

Alfred Barnard is not noted for his humour, usually being more absorbed with the dimensions of mash tuns and capacities of wash stills than with any more social aspects of whisky-making. The 'whisky city' of Campbeltown did, however, seduce him into a moment of levity, and he tells the following tale.

'A capital story is told of an aged woman who resided near Hazelburn. She was a rather doubtful character and was charged before the sheriff with smuggling. The charge being held proven, it fell to his lordship to pronounce sentence. When about to do so, he thus addressed the culprit, "I daresay my poor woman it is not often that you have been guilty of this fault".

' "Deed no Sheriff," she readily replied. "I haena made a drap since youn wee keg I sent to yersel'".'

One excise officer in the Glenlivet area was dismissed during the 1820s for growing his own grain and selling it to illicit whisky-makers.

The story is told of an old Highland illicit distiller who appeared before the local magistrate on a charge of illegally making whisky, having been caught with a still in his possession. The Highlander insisted that he had never used the still, but the magistrate replied that he had been caught with the equipment necessary for distilling in his possession, and that was enough as far as the law was concerned.

'In that case,' said the Highlander, 'I'd like several cases of rape to be taken into account when you pass sentence.'

'So are you admitting that you are guilty of rape?' asked the magistrate. 'No', replied the Highlander, 'but I have the necessary equipment.'

Although illicit distilling in Scotland largely died out during the nineteenth century, a few stills survived until much later, and doubtless some still survive. In Ireland, poitin production remains a thriving part of the black economy.

In 1998 a whisky-distilling operation was discovered in the unlikely setting of a workshop unit on Dundee's North Tayworks Industrial Estate. A locksmith discovered a still, boilers and hundreds of empty bottles when he called to change the locks after the tenant fell behind with his rent payments. The tenant, unsurprisingly, could not be traced, having taken to the hills and glens of Angus ahead of the modern-day gaugers.

According to a car mechanic who rented the unit next to the 'distillery', 'There were two men used to come about the place but they never had much to say for themselves. They seemed to do all their work at night and they never seemed to take any deliveries during daylight hours. Now I can understand why.'

'On Skye, you can still see the burn marks around a telephone pole, the result of someone's ill-fated attempt to bend red-hot copper pipe into a condensing worm.'
TOM MORTON.

'At Callyhill John Ennery has a seat; it lies at a small distance on ye left of ye great Road, in a fine sporting country; brush woods abound in ye part. There are neither inns nor Alehouses on Ys road, yet almost every house have for public Sale Aquavitae or Whiskey, which is greatly esteemed by ye Inhabitants, as a wholesome balsamic Diuretic; they take it here in common before their Meals. To make it the more agreeable they fill an iron pot with ys spirit, putting sugar, mint and butter and when it hath seethed for some time they fill their square cans which they call Meathers and this drink out then to each other. What is surprising they will drink it to Intoxication and are never sick after it neither doth it impair their health.'

BUTLER'S *JOURNEY THROUGH FERMANAGH* (1760).

Irish playwright, drinker, republican, and all-round anti-establishment figure Brendan Behan perhaps surprisingly was not a devotee of the illegal stuff. He wrote of poitin 'No matter what anyone tells you about the fine old drop of the mountain dew, it stands to sense that a few old men sitting up in the back of a haggard in the mountains with milk churns and all sorts of improvised apparatus cannot hope to make good spirit.'

Perhaps Behan's opinion of poitin was influenced by sampling 'prison poitin' in the Curragh internment camp during the Second World War. Behan was renowned within the camp for his laziness, and he developed the habit of relieving himself into empty bottles which he proceeded to throw out of the window in order to eliminate the tiresome business of getting out of bed. Empty bottles for the poitin which was ingeniously distilled by the internees to celebrate Christmas in 1943 were obviously in short supply, and Behan was duly presented with his share of the poitin in a 'recycled' bottle that had been retrieved from below his window.

The story is told of a West Cork man who, during the struggle for Irish independence, in 1920 or 1921, ran his motorbike on poitin when petrol was at a premium, and then siphoned off a nightcap from the fuel tank when he got home.

The romance of poitin is spoilt slightly by a warning issued by the police to present and prospective customers of a remote illicit distillery in County Donegal in April 1999 when dead rats were discovered in a vat of poitin during a raid.

'Sure, it goes down your throat like a torchlight procession.'
ANONYMOUS POITIN DRINKER.

Come gaugers all from Donegal,
From Sligo and Leitrim too,
Oh we'll give them the slip
And take a sip of the rare ould mountain dew...

...There's a neat little still
At the foot of the hill
Where the smoke curls up to the sky.
By a whiff of the smell
You can plainly tell
That there's poitin, boys, close by.

'*The Rare Ould Mountain Dew*' (trad.)

Until 1855 the levels of duty differed quite dramatically in England and Scotland, which led to cross-border smuggling on a major scale. In 1830 the Excise Board set up a sixty-strong special force to help prevent this lucrative trade, and when the Newcastle-Edinburgh railway line opened, excise officers searched luggage at Berwick and Carlisle for contraband bottles.

During the 1820s up to 11,000 gallons of Scotch whisky was illegally imported into England each week, and one particularly cunning ruse adopted by smugglers was to train dogs to swim across the border rivers of the Eden and the Esk, carrying pigs' bladders filled with spirit.

Sir Archibald Geikle (*Scottish Reminiscences*, 1904) wrote 'Whisky was then contraband, and liable to extra duty when taken into England. At that time, this liquor was hardly known south of the Tweed, save to the Scots who imported it from their native country.'

Illicit whisky-making not only took place in Scotland, but south of the border as well. Lanty Slee and Moses Rigg were notorious Victorian

Lake District distillers, while it is claimed that 21 illegal distilleries were discovered in the Lancashire town of Bolton between 1835 and 1837.

In Northumberland, illicit whisky was known as 'innocent', because it was innocent of the payment of excise duty.

The suppression of illicit distilling was one thing, but in 1919 the government of the USA went a radical step further, and suppressed the production and consumption of all alcohol. That was the theory, at any rate. Prohibition in the USA lasted until the Volstead Act was repealed in 1933.

Consumption of illegal alcohol was so widespread in the USA during Prohibition that it was almost impossible for the State to persuade juries to convict defendants in court cases concerning production and supply of drink. Out of 2,739 cases brought during 1923, only 277 resulted in convictions!

In 1930 no fewer than 282,122 stills were discovered in the USA.

'There were 32,000 speakeasies in New York during Prohibition, as opposed to only 15,000 official bars before the Volstead Act rang the curtain down on legal imbibing.' TOM MORTON.

'Once, during Prohibition, I was forced to live for days on nothing but food and water.'   WC FIELDS.

Samuel Bronfman gained respectability as the President of Seagram Distillers, which his family took over in the late 1920s. By that time the Bronfmans had already made a great deal of money by illegally running Canadian whisky into the 'dry' USA. The gangster 'Lucky' Luciano claimed that Bronfman was '...bootleggin' enough whisky across the Canadian border to double the size of Lake Erie!'

One trick employed by the Bronfman organisation was to throw sacks filled with bottles of whisky over the side of boats if they were being pursued by coastguard officers. Attached to the sacks were large blocks of salt, and the sacks and salt duly sank without trace. After a few hours, however, the salt dissolved and the sacks of whisky floated to the surface. All that was needed to retrieve them was a compass reference taken at the time the contraband was jettisoned.

Writing of the West Highlands of Scotland during the nineteenth century, Ian MacDonald noted 'The Loch Druing smugglers are said to have frequently sunk their still in the loch, attaching a cord and small float, by which it could be hauled out when required.'

Captain William McCoy specialised in running Cutty Sark Scotch whisky into the USA on board his clipper, the *Arethusa*. Unlike many smugglers, he always provided quality merchandise, hence the expression 'The Real McCoy'.

The US market was too large and too lucrative for Scotch distillers to abandon due to the small matter of Prohibition. They continued to supply the States, determined to maintain a high profile there, so that once Prohibition was repealed, legal exports could continue as before.

Many Scotch whisky companies set up agencies in Canada, Bermuda, Cuba, the Bahamas, and even the tiny French colonial islands of St Pierre and Miquelon, off Nova Scotia. These agencies legally imported vast quantities of Scotch, which were then shipped close to the US coast. Provided they stayed in international waters (ie 12 miles or more offshore) they were breaking no laws. 'Bootleggers' duly came out in fast boats and purchased cases of whisky, which they then ran ashore.

In 1922 St Pierre and Miquelon imported over 116,000 gallons of whisky. Had it all been for bona fide consumption, then these were colonies with a fearsome drink problem. The two islands had a combined population of some 6,000 people, which meant that every person, adult and child, would have had to consume 20 gallons of whisky that year!

Scotland's smallest legal distillery at Edradour in Perthshire played an unlikely role in the Prohibition-busting business. Edradour was owned by William Whiteley – the 'dean of distillers' – and his King's Ransom blend was a favourite in the USA during the dry years. It was fired onto Long Island beaches in hollow torpedoes by prominent underworld figures like Frank Costello, who also used a seaplane and a former German U-boat to guarantee delivery of whisky. Costello is rumoured to have funded the US company which subsequently took over Whiteley's business.

The bootleggers were sophisticated and ruthless in defence of their lucrative activity. On one occasion the US Coastguard Commander Thomas Baker brought his destroyer alongside a boat which he suspected to be loaded with bootleg whiskey. The teetotal Baker had a reputation for being somewhat trigger-happy, and was known to sink bootleggers' vessels without compunction. This time, before he could give the order to fire, a seaplane appeared and laid down a smokescreen between the Commander's vessel and the second boat. A few seconds later an elderly submarine surfaced and shot the twin screws off Baker's destroyer!

The great Victorian whisky entrepreneur Tommy Dewar was travelling by train through a dry state of Canada during the 1920s. When he asked how it might be possible for him to obtain a drink he was advised by the conductor to try his luck at a store the next time the train stopped. Dewar duly did this, but on asking for a bottle of whisky he was asked by the storekeeper 'Are you sick, mister, or got a medical certificate?'

'No.'

'Then I can't do it; but I reckon our cholera mixture'll about fix you. Try a bottle of that.'

Dewar was handed a bottle which on one side carried a label stating 'Cholera Mixture: a wineglassful to be taken every two hours or oftener if required.' On the other was the familiar label of his family's blended whisky.

Dewar drank the bottle, and never did contract cholera.

In November 1929 six Kentucky distilleries were licensed to produce whiskey for medicinal purposes. Operating as the American Medicinal Liquor Company they proceeded to keep doctors busy by producing 1.4m US gallons per year of 'medicinal' bourbon.

In 1922 Chicago doctors prescribed some 200,000 gallons of 'medicinal' spirit.

Prohibition was not limited to the USA, and British temperance activites led to a little-known period of official drouth in the Caithness fishing port of Wick.

Wick was the old herring capital of Scotland, and during the nineteenth and early twentieth centuries it gained an unenviable reputation for lawlessness, as large numbers of migrant workers decended on the borough during the herring season.

In the 1840s a Presbyterian minister noted of Wick that '...the herring fishing has increased wealth, but also wickedness. No care is taken of the 10,000 strangers of both sexes who are crowded together with the inhabitants in the narrow streets of Wick during the six weeks of the fishery. There is great consumption of spirits, there being 22 public houses in Wick and 23 in Pulteneytown...Seminaries of Satan and Belial.' More than 500 gallons of whisky was reputed to be drunk in the port during this period per day.

Such historic excesses doubtless helped the 'dry' cause, and Wick's period of Prohibition lasted from 1922 until 1947 – eleven years longer than the better documented 'experiment' on the other side of the Atlantic. During that time, at least two whisky stills operated in the town, along with a number of drinking dens. According to Caithness historian Iain Sutherland (*Vote No Licence*) '...the most daring of all operated in a restaurant, whose regulars knew that when the fancy silver teapot was in use, that its contents had been brewed some considerable time previously. And not in India or China either.'

Harry Harrison Kroll offers a uniquely personal view of Prohibition in the USA, from time spent as a teacher 'in a mountain school.'

'Half of the men, old and young, were more or less drunk; most of the callow youths were drinking or trying to act drunk; and the close room with the old potbellied stove cranking out heat made just about the most nauseating odor I'd ever smelt. But not quite. Somebody – I laid it on old Gus Buelar who was my school trustee – emitted a deep abdominal explosion that knocked me back on my heels. It was the most ghastly stench I'd ever known. It was all laced with whisky. I think there were sweet potatoes there, and hog meat, and moonshine whisky. Legal whisky could never have stunk like that.'

Aeneas Macdonald, writing during Prohibition, but from the other side of the Atlantic to Kroll noted 'When the United States will manufacture whisky (or at least a liquid whose local name was whisky) a pleasing concoction called 'Bourbon oil' was sometimes added to give it a frothy appearance. Bourbon oil consists of fusel oil, acetate of potassium, sulphuric acid, and other equally attractive ingredients. If such things could be done before Prohibition, one need not be surprised at anything that happens after.'

Some bad and some lethal 'whiskeys' were produced during Prohibition, with rotting cactuses being favoured by Mexican 'distillers'.

'Prohibition has added two more names to the nomenclature of whisky: "Squirrel" whisky, so called because it induces in its devotees an irresistible desire to climb trees, and "Rabbit" whisky which creates an impulse to leap and run.'

AENEAS MACDONALD.

'...the American experiment proved that you cannot legislate a people into sobriety...'

NEIL GUNN.

Tourist (who has been refreshing himself with the toddy of the country):
'I shay, ole fler! Highlands seem to 'gree with you wonerfly – annomishtake.
Why, you look DOUBLE the man already!'

Chapter 4
Selling it

During the last two decades of the nineteenth century blended whisky became a drink for the world – creating large fortunes for its leading proponents along the way. The development of the art of blending whisky fortuitously coincided with the devastation of the French grape crop due to the phylloxera louse. Scotch whisky was no longer perceived as a variable and frequently forbidding drink from the savage Highlands, unsuitable for the delicate palates of Lowlanders and sassenachs. It had graduated to being a fit replacement for brandy on the tables of the great and the good.

'My father could never have drunk whisky except when shooting on a moor or in some very dull chilly place. He lived in the age of brandy and soda.'
WINSTON CHURCHILL.

An apocryphal story is told of rival Perth whisky magnates Arthur Bell and John Dewar. Finding themselves with time to spare before a church meeting, the pair adjourned to a local hotel for a quick spot of refreshment.

'What will you have?' asked Bell.

'A Bell's,' replied Dewar. 'It wouldn't do to go into the meeting smelling of whisky.'

Tommy Dewar set out for London in 1885, aged just 21, with the intention of making Dewar's White Label blended whisky known beyond the bounds of Scotland. Dewar was fond of telling the story of how he arrived in the Metropolis with two business introductions. One turned out to be dead and the other bankrupt. Dewar was not deterred, however, and began to 'cold sell' his whisky around the capital.

In 1886 he caused uproar at the Brewers' Show in the Agricultural Hall by advertising Dewar's whisky with the aid of a piper in full Highland dress. The other exhibitors were furious, but Tommy Dewar refused to stop the deafening music. The story found its way into the newspapers, giving Dewar invaluable publicity.

Dewar was friendly with fellow Scottish entrepreneur Thomas Lipton, who was popularly known as 'Tea Tom', just as Dewar became known as 'Whisky Tom.' Both men were batchelors, and during one trip to Central America Dewar wired his friend with the message 'You can buy three wives here for six pounds of Lipton's tea. Why not come out?'

Lipton replied 'I am sending out the tea. Send samples of wives.'

Once, at a smart dinner party, he was introduced to a woman who rather haughtily announced that her name was 'Porter-Porter, with a hyphen.'

'And mine', he replied, 'is Dewar-Dewar, with a syphon.'

He became famous for his 'Dewarisms', which included 'Do right and fear no man. Don't write and fear no woman.' Another was 'If you do not advertise, you fossilise.' Dewar certainly took his own advice to heart, having an enormous neon image of a piper erected on the side of the Old Shot Tower near Waterloo Bridge. Periodically, the piper lifted a glass of Dewars to his lips – his kilt and beard swaying as he did so.

'A teetotaller is one who suffers from thirst instead of enjoying it.'

TOMMY DEWAR.

One of Tommy Dewar's great professional rivals was James Buchanan, of Black & White whisky fame. In 1922 he received a peerage, becoming Lord Woolavington. This peerage was acquired in return for a contribution to Prime Minister Lloyd George's Liberal party coffers, as was the custom at the time. Distrusting the 'Welsh Wizard', who had proved himself to be no friend to the Scotch whisky industry, Buchanan chose his new title and then signed the cheque for his 'donation' with the name Lord Woolavington, so that it could not be cashed until his elevation was a fait accompli.

While Chancellor of the Exchequer, David Lloyd George increased duty on Scotch whisky by a third in his 'People's Budget' of 1909. 'Whisky Baron' Peter Mackie of the 'White Horse' whisky company retorted '...what can one expect of a Welsh country solicitor being placed, without any commercial training, as Chancellor of the Exchequer in a large country like this?'

Determined to secure the concession to supply blended whisky to one of the foremost London hotels, James Buchanan hired a dozen out of work young actors, had them dressed immaculately for dinner, and reserved a table in the hotel's dining room for a banquet.

The eye-catching group duly arrived in the dining room and took their places at the table. When the wine waiter arrived to ask them what they would like to drink one of them asked for 'The Buchanan Blend.' The other eleven all said they would like the same. When the waiter admitted that the hotel didn't stock the brand, the dozen actors rose as one, chorused 'What! No Buchanan's?' and immediately left the hotel. An order was placed with Buchanan the following day.

Tommy Dewar was knighted in 1901, and in 1919 he became Baron Dewar of Homestall. He lived the life of an English country squire in deepest Sussex, and was a notable breeder of racehorses. His brother, John, had become the first of the so-called 'Whisky Barons' when he was created Lord Forteviot of Dupplin in 1916. In addition to Buchanan, Peter Mackie was made a baronet, and Alexander Walker of

Johnnie Walker was knighted.

When John and Tommy Dewar's father, John, died in 1880 the annual profits of John Dewar & Sons stood at £1,321. When the brothers died within six months of each other in 1930 they left estates totalling in excess of £10 million.

'Whisky barons bought country estates just as yuppies buy Barbour jackets.'
PIP HILLS, SCOTS ON SCOTCH (1991).

Tommy Dewar was probably the most energetic of the blended whisky evangelists, visiting 26 countries and appointing 32 agents during a two-year world tour in the 1890s, while Charles Gordon of Wm Grant & Sons showed extraordinary determination and resilience in making 180 calls before achieving his first sale. Once into his stride, Gordon couldn't stop selling whisky, and in 1909-10 he visited India, Malaya, Australia and New Zealand on sales trips, and by 1914 Grant's had established 60 agencies in more than 30 countries.

Adam Teacher, of William Teacher & Sons, had experienced a less successful sales trip in 1871, when he chose to travel to South America on board the *Tumuri*, a vessel carrying a cargo of guano, whose captain was drunk more often he was sober. In Montevideo Teacher spent most of his time managing to avoid business of any kind outwith theatres and billiards-halls, but on the way home lack of food meant that he was forced to eat sheep's head broth, and at one stage the ship was hit by a hurricane. This was followed by a near-mutiny, and finally a shipwreck. There is no record of the number of orders for

Teacher's whisky which Adam took during his South American expedition.

At the close of the nineteenth century the boom in blended whisky turned to bust, and one of the highest-profile victims was the Leith firm of Pattison's Ltd. Pattison's went into liquidation in 1899, with liabilities of more than £500,000, and assets of less than half that amount. This was a massive bankruptcy for the time, and the Pattison brothers, Robert and Walter, both went on to serve prison sentences for fraud.

The Pattisons had developed a cavalier disregard for the finer points of accounting, and even for many of the cruder ones, and their rise to prominence was accompanied by marketing gimmicks that would have made even Tommy Dewar blush.

The brothers once paid for 500 parrots to be trained to squawk 'Drink Pattisons' Whisky', and they also produced a blended whisky to commemorate the death of General Gordon at Khartoum in 1885. Considering the amount of cheap grain whisky and the tiny quantities of malt that went into their profit-maximising blends, this could be considered bad taste in both senses!

No fewer than 21 new distilleries had been constructed on Speyside alone during the 1890s boom years, and 'bust' led to a sudden cessation in building projects. It is said that when Glen Elgin was completed in 1900 many of the tradesmen who had been employed on the project went unpaid. The steeplejacks who had built the distillery chimney only received their dues because they threatened to dismantle the structure if cash was not forthcoming.

Before becoming an actor, David Niven worked as a salesman in the USA for Ballantine's whisky.

In the mid 1990s Quentin Crisp Single Cask Whisky was launched, designed for sale in gay bars and clubs in Edinburgh, Glasgow and London. Reports that the makers of Highland Queen were concerned about a potential fall in sales were never officially confirmed.

Following United Distillers' decision – after careful consideration – not to specifically target the gay market during the late 1990s, *Duty-Free News* ran an April 1st spoof feature on the subject. It 'revealed' that UD was about to launch Johnnie Walker Pink Label. Instead of the traditional top hat and white jodhpurs, the famous 'striding man' would wear a string vest and tight leather trousers. The project, claimed *Duty Free News*, was codenamed Johnnie Mincer, and the early marketing would be done in San Francisco and Sydney, where the new advertising catch line would be revealed. It was to be 'You'll feel like a new man'.

For the uninitiated, attempting to pronounce the names of malt whiskies can be quite traumatic. Some are deceptive. Glenmorangie looks quite straightforward, but just where does the stress go? I've always found Glenmorangie reduces stress, but that's just me.

One man who is subjected to more bad stabs at whisky names

than most is Richard Joynson of Loch Fyne Whiskies, who reckons that the Scotch whisky industry is unique in that it sells products with names which no one can spell and very few are able to pronounce. His company operates a popular mail order business and also welcomes visitors from all over the world to its shop in the picturesque Argyllshire village of Inveraray. Generous fellow that he is, Richard promises customers purchasing whisky as a gift that if it's not appreciated by the recipient the Loch Fyne staff will finish it for them if they simply return the bottle. That's what I call service.

According to Richard, 'We often get asked for a bottle of Leapfrog, when the customer means Laphroaig, though to be fair it's been known in the industry as Leapfrog for a long time, and even blenders tend to call it that before using its real name. Murray McDavid now bottle it under the name Leapfrog! We once received a faxed order from Japan asking for "Laphloaig" and "Longlow".

'One lady recently referred to it as Lappydoodah, while the Gaelic blend Te Bheag (*chay-vek*) not surprisingly often becomes Tea Bag. Antiquary is Aunty Mary, and Bunnahabhain (*boon-a-haavun*) is always known to our staff as Bunny. Longmorn is frequently Longhorn. One of my favourites is Sheep Dip. A few weeks ago I distinctly heard a customer ask for a bottle of Sheep's Dick.'

Switching to music hall mode, Richard recalls a customer requesting a Pig's Nose. 'Why, madam?' he replied, 'there doesn't look much wrong with the one you've got.' In similar vein, 'Have you got Stag's Breath?' 'No sir, I brush my teeth twice a day.'

One of the most frequent queries at Loch Fyne Whiskies' shop is, 'Have you sampled all the whiskies you have on sale?' Richard's reply is, 'We keep trying to, but it always gets to the point where we know there are three we still haven't tasted, but by that time we're too pissed to remember which ones they are, so we have to start all over again.'

A few years ago the upmarket London store of Fortnum & Mason had a bottle of Springbank single malt whisky on display. This was no ordinary Springbank, however, as it dated from 1919, and was worth around £7,500.

One day the bottle was stolen, and when the story got to the press, Gordon Wright of Springbank was asked for his comments. He replied that Springbank was an ideal accompaniment to most food, but in this instance the thieves would probably be best with fish and chips. The display bottle contained malt vinegar.

The distillation of whisky, or whiskey, is usually associated with a handful of countries. Scotland, Ireland, the USA, Canada, and Japan spring most readily to mind. So it may come as a surprise to discover that whisk(e)y is currently also produced in the Czech Republic, Spain, Turkey and Pakistan.

In Pakistan, whisky is distilled by the Murree Brewery Co Ltd at Rawalpindi, where temperatures are so high that the wash stills stand in the open air, and maturation takes place in cellars rather than warehouses!

Unusual 'world whiskies' surface from time to time. In 1998 Christie's Glasgow auction house sold a bottle of early twentieth century Italian whisky, described as being 'made of naturally dried distillates of fruits and aromatic herbs.'

At the same auction, a bottle of Australian malt whisky was offered for sale. Whisky from 'Down Under', blended or malt, may be rare in the northern hemisphere, but the country has a domestic whisky-distilling industry dating back to the 1860s, and provided Scotch whisky with its most important export market until the Second World War. Today Australian whisky is only produced on the island of Tasmania, where two small, independent distilleries were founded during the 1990s.

If Australian whiskies remain elusive, single malt from New Zealand is quite easy to find in Britain. Lammerlaw single malt whisky is made in Dunedin, at the southernmost distillery in the world, and it finds its way onto the shelves of retail chains like Oddbins for the simple reason that both Wilson's distillery in Dunedin and the Oddbins chain are owned by the giant Seagram organisation. Oddbins can boast of stocking single malts from the most southerly and most northerly working whisky distilleries in the world. The northernmost is Orkney's Highland Park.

Dunedin was the first settlement of Scottish immigrants in New Zealand, and South Island offers good conditions for whisky making, with pure, soft water supplies, quality barley, and even peat. Unfortunately, the distillery's designers chose to construct their still from stainless steel rather than copper, and the spirit subsequently produced became a by-word for bad whisky all over New Zealand. The make of Wilson's distillery improved dramatically after Seagram acquired it and installed a copper condenser on the highly unorthodox still.

Many nations have tried to copy Scotch and Irish whisk(e)y, and none more determinedly than the Japanese. One English-born former Tokyo resident recalled being asked in the 1920s by a local whisky distiller to come up with a label which would lull drinkers into believing that they were getting genuine Scotch. He suggested 'Guaranteed bottled in Buckingham Palace under the personal supervision of His Majesty the King.' The labels were duly printed and the whisky went on sale.

The Japanese renamed a town Aberdeen so that they could label the whisky produced there as 'Blended and bottled in Aberdeen', thereby appearing to give it a Scottish provenance, but without actually breaking any laws or telling any lies.

Stories are told of early Japanese whiskies with names such as King Anne, and King Victoria's Sporran, but a personal favourite concerns a whisky produced in Ecuador. One can only conjecture about the origins of the name, and speculate that perhaps a disgruntled expatriate Scotsman was asked to help choose something suitable. The whisky is marketed as 'Auld Piss'.

The days when unscrupulous producers tried to pass their local spirit off as Scotch whisky are largely gone, due in part to the tireless efforts of the Scotch Whisky Association. In 1984 some 22,500 cases of whisky labelled as Johnnie Walker were intercepted at an airport in Italy, en route from Bulgaria. The labels were adequate counterfeits, except that they lacked the legend 'Produce of Scotland'.

'I am sorry I missed the bizarre experience of a friend of mine who was offered a whisky with the name King Edward the First while visiting Vienna...The most atrocious fluid that I have seen masquerading under the name Scotch was in Denmark.'

JAMES ROSS.

'Scotch Whisky, made in Germany, is now being largely imported into India. The wholesale price is sixpence per quart bottle.'

Vanity Fair (December 1892).

Whisky being the global drink that it is, and Scotland being at the centre of the whisky universe, many Scottish distilleries receive large numbers of foreign visitors, keen to experience the mysteries of distillation. The following story comes from Jim Turle of the Edrington Group, and concerns Glengoyne Distillery in Stirlingshire:

'We had a party of Russian VIPs touring Glengoyne one day, and the guide, Heather, took them to look at the picturesque waterfall which flows behind the distillery. Suddenly one of the Russians stripped to his underpants and leapt into the pool at the foot of the waterfall, and proceeded to swim energetically around it. Mindful of the insurance implications and possible international repercussions if he drowned, Heather turned to one of the party and begged him to persuade his comrade to get out of the water. The Russian shook his head sorrowfully. "I'm a sergeant," he told her. "He's a general."

Happily, the officer survived his swim, and there were no lurid newspaper headlines about "Russian General Drowns in Scottish Distillery".'

The Scotch Whisky Association exists, in its own words, '...to promote Scotch Whisky and to protect the interests of the Scotch Whisky Industry'.

Campbell Evans of The Scotch Whisky Association tells the tale of an influential Japanese journalist with whom he spent a week touring a variety of Scottish distilleries.

'From the second night onwards, the journalist spent a large portion of each evening in his hotel room. Was he conducting a secret tasting, or sampling the whiskies from the distilleries he had visited, I wondered. Had he discovered the mystery of Scotch? It was only later, on returning to the hotel in which we had spent our first night, that I discovered my Japanese companion had been labouring hard at his Japanese-English dictionary, constructing a letter and a series of complex sketches with lengthy captions. This he had subsequently posted to the owner of the hotel. None of the drawings had much to do with distilleries, but were a painstaking sequence of pictures which consisted of a hotel lobby, hotel corridor, hotel bedroom door, hotel bedroom interior, and lastly a very detailed sketch of a hotel bed, complete with cross-section of the mattress. A large red arrow pointed to the area between the bed-base and the mattress. The accompanying caption read, "Japanese journalist use this as trouser press and forgot trousers. Enclosed is £40.00. Please send trousers to following Tokyo address..."

Housekeeper: 'Losh me, Laird, ye'll no have asket all thae folks to stop the nicht? There isna beds for the half o' them.'

Laird: 'Hoots, woman! dinna fash yersel. Gie them plenty whisky and they'll find beds themsels.'

Chapter 5
Writing
about it

Irish playright Brendan Behan reckoned that he was 'a drinker with a writing problem', and he was one among many. Some of the twentieth century's most talented American novelists, dramatists and poets were associated with excessive imbibing: Scott Fitzgerald, Robert Lowell, Ernest Hemingway, Eugene O'Neill, Tennessee Williams and Jack Kerouac to name but ten. The Welsh poet Dylan Thomas is almost as well-known for his consumption of alcohol as he is for his verse. It was Thomas who said 'An alcoholic is someone you don't like who drinks as much as you do.'

Whether they drank because they were writers or wrote because they were drinkers is best left to academics and pyschologists to muse upon.

Whisky figures in a great deal of fiction, drama and poetry, and as in 'real life', it is sometimes a force for good, and sometimes a force for evil.

The most celebrated literary liason with whisky occurs in Compton Mackenzie's comic masterpiece *Whisky Galore*, published in 1947, and subsequently made into a highly successful film. In the novel, the fictional vessel the SS *Cabinet Minister* is wrecked off the Hebridean island of Little Todday during the Second World War, and the action centres on the subsequent 'salvage' of much of its cargo of whisky by islanders, for whom wartime rationing has meant a terrible lack of the cratur. Whisky has a medicinal role here, for the local GP, Doctor Mclaren, has no doubts that only whisky can sufficiently raise the spirits of his patient Hector MacRurie if a terminal decline is to be prevented. The death of Captain MacPhee is directly attributed to his horror at discovering there is no whisky left on the island.

'Love makes the world go round?' asks Norman Macleod rhetorically, 'Not at all. Whisky makes it go round twice as fast.'

The events of *Whisky Galore* were inspired by the real life wrecking of the SS *Politician* off the island of Eriskay in the Outer Hebrides in 1941. Part of its cargo was 24,000 tons of spirits, and the islanders enthusiastically looted it, hiding bottles in peat bogs, haystacks, drain pipes and even in babies' cots.

In addition to the whisky, the cargo included bathroom fittings, perfume, and cosmetics, and such items did not escape the attentions of the looters, even if whisky was their principal preoccupation.

One islander recalled visiting his neighbour soon after the wreck, only to find him sitting among a top-of-the-range bathroom suite, complete with luxury bath, cabinets, basin and lavatory in his croft, despite the fact that no houses on the island were equipped with mains water. Bottles of whisky of every conceivable brand lined the shelves, and, according to the neighbour 'The hens kept coming in, and he'd spray coluds of perfume to keep them out. It was a crazy time, just crazy.'

If Mackenzie makes humorous capital out of a 'whisky wreck', then a more sober account of the realities of such events comes from the *Argyllshire Herald* of 27 May 1859, as dicovered by Murdo MacDonald, archivist for Argyll & Bute District Council.

'The brig *Mary Ann*, of Greenock, now lying a wreck at Kilchoman Bay, Islay, is fast breaking up, and portions of the cargo floating ashore. Up to Saturday there had been about 200 boxes saved, containing bottled brandy, whisky, and gin, and upwards of six puncheons of whisky, brandy, and wine; but the wildest scenes of drunkenness and riot that can be imagined took place. Hundreds of people flocked from all parts of the neighbourhood, especially the Portnahaven fishermen, who turned out to a man. Boxes were seized as soon as landed, broken up, and the contents carried away and drunk. Numbers could be seen here and there lying amongst the rocks, unable to move, while others were fighting like savages. Sergeant Kennedy and constable Chisholm, of the County Police, were in attendance, and used every means in their power to put a stop to the work of pillage. They succeeded in keeping some order during the day of Thursday, but when night came on the natives showed evident symptoms of their disapproval of the police being there at all, and on the latter preventing a fellow from knocking the end out of a puncheon, in order, as he said, to "treat all hands", they were immediately seized upon by the mob, and a hand to hand fight ensued, which lasted half an hour, and ended in the defeat of the police, of whom there were only two against from 30 to 40 of the natives. The police beat a retreat to Cuil Farm – about a mile from the scene of action – closely pursued by about 30 of the natives, yelling like savages. Mrs Simpson of Cuil, on seeing the state of matters, took the police into the house and secured the doors, at the same time placing arms at their disposal for their protection. The mob yelled two or three times round the house, but learning that the police had got fire-arms, they left and returned to the beach. Next morning the scene presented was still more frightful to contemplate. In one place there lay stretched the dead body of a large and powerful man. Donald M'Phayden, a fisherman from Portnahaven, who was considered the strongest man in Islay; but the brandy proved to be still stronger. He has left a wife and family. Others apparently in a dying state were being conveyed to the nearest houses, where every means were used to save life. Mrs Simpson, who is a very kind and humane person, supplied every remedy, but there was no medical man within fifteen or sixteen miles of the place. Mr James Simpson got a coffin made for M'Phayden, and had him interred on Friday. At the time when the corpse was being taken away, some groups could be seen fighting, others dancing, and others craving for drink, in order, as they said, to bury the man decently. Up to Saturday there was only one death, but on Monday it was reported that two more had died.'

In Sir Walter Scott's novel *St Ronans Well* (1824), Sir Bingo treats the Doctor and the Captain to a cordial prepared in Glenlivet. The Captain's reaction to tasting it was to say 'By Cot, it is the only liquor fit for a gentleman to drink in the morning, if he can have the good fortune to come by it, you see.'

The doctor's verdict was 'It is worth all the wines of France for flavour, and more cordial to the system besides.'

'Phairson had a son
Who married Noah's daughter,
And nearly spoilt the flood
By trinking up ta water.
Which he would have done –
I, at least, believe it –
Had ta mixture been
Only half Glenlivet.'

FROM '*THE MASSACRE OF MACPHERSON*'
BY WILLIAM AYTOUN.

The English-born novelist and humorist Mark Twain was very fond of whiskey, and when visiting Britain he was once stopped by customs officers who enquired about the contents of his luggage. Twain replied that his bags contained nothing but clothing. One of the customs officers opened a bag, and discovered a bottle of whiskey. 'Officer', said Twain, 'for me whiskey is clothing.'

'Give an Irishman lager for a month and he's a dead man. An Irishman is lined with copper and the beer corrodes it. But whiskey polishes the copper and is the saving of him.' MARK TWAIN, *LIFE ON THE MISSISSIPPI* (1833).

It was Twain, too, whose views on aspects of the US political scene were summed up in the phrase 'Whiskey is taken into the [congressional] committee rooms in demijohns and carried out in demagogues.'

'The steward placed on his table a syphon and a bottle of whisky which carried the label Edouard VIII: very old Genuine Scotch Whisky: Andre Bloc and Cie, Saigon, and the coloured picture of a Regency buck, gazing sceptically at the consumer through a quizzing glass.

    ' "Alphonse", said Corker, "I'm surprised at you".

    ' "No like?"

    ' "Bloody well no like".'

EVELYN WAUGH, SCOOP (1938).

It seems unlikely that the makers of The Macallan would approve of the method of experiencing their whisky as related by Alan Warner in his 1995 novel *Morvern Callar*. For one thing, it makes all that business about maturing it exclusively in ex-sherry casks seem rather academic.

    '...for a crack me and Mockit injected whisky into each other's temples, Macallan twelve-year-old of course. I love the subtle smokiness of the Macallan. We were steaming out the mind totally mortal within ten seconds.'

And purists agonise over which brand of spring water best accompanies their favourite malt...

'There is no such thing as a large whiskey.'

OLIVER ST JOHN GOGARTY.

'If an angel out of heaven
gives you something else to drink
thank her for her kind intention
and pour it down the sink.'

GK CHESTERTON ON WHISKY.

'They are not a drunken race but no man is so abstemious as to refuse the morning dram, which they call a skalk.'

DR SAMUEL JOHNSON, *A JOURNEY TO THE WESTERN ISLES OF SCOTLAND* (1775).

James Boswell wrote in *The Journal of a Tour to the Hebrides* (1784) of Samuel Johnson's first encounter with whisky. It took place in an Inveraray inn: 'We supped well; and after supper, Dr. Johnson, whom I had not seen taste any fermented liquor during all our travels, called for a gill of whisky.

"Come (said he) let me know what it is that makes a Scotchman happy!"

'He drank it all but a drop, which I begged him leave to pour into my glass that I might say we had drunk whisky together. I proposed Mrs Thrale should be our toast. He would not have her drank in whisky, but rather some insular lady; so we drank, I think, Miss Macpherson.'

'*The word whisky signifies water, and is applied by way of eminence to strong water, or distilled liquor. The spirit drunk in the North is drawn from barley. I never tasted it, except once for experiment at the inn in Inverary, when I thought it preferable to any English malt brandy. It was strong, but not pungent, and was free from the empyreumatick taste or smell. What was the process I had no opportunity of inquiring, nor do I wish to improve the art of making poison pleasant.*'   DR SAMUEL JOHNSON.

'*Oats, n.s. A grain, which in England is generally given to horses, but in Scotland supports the people.*'
       DR SAMUEL JOHNSON, *DICTIONARY OF THE ENGLISH LANGUAGE* (1755).

'*Drinking is in reality an occupation which employs a considerable portion of the time of many people; and to conduct it in the most rational and agreeable manner is one of the great arts of living*'   JAMES BOSWELL (1740-95).

The novelist George Douglas Brown clearly belonged to the school of thought that recognised whisky as a force for ill. In his novel *The House with the Green Shutters* (1901) the heavy-drinking John Gourlay gets 'Dutch courage' in the bar of the Red Lion before confronting and murdering his father. After this, he, his mother, and his sister proceed to commit suicide.

> 'With shaking knees Gourlay advanced to the bar, and, "For God's sake, Aggie", he whispered, "Give me a Kinblythmont!"
> It went at a gulp.
> ' "Another!" he gasped, like a man dying of thirst, whom his first sip maddens for more. "Another! Another!"'.

In another passage, John Gourlay tells Deacon Allardyce that his favourite blend is the fictional 'Kinblythmont's Cure', though he also favours Anderson's Sting o'Delight and 'Balsillie's Brig o'the Mains.'

'Whiskey to breakfast, whiskey to dinner, whiskey to supper; whiskey when you meet a friend, whiskey over all business meetings whatsoever; whiskey before you go into the kirk, whiskey when you come out; whiskey when you are about to take a journey, whiskey all along the road, whiskey at the journey's end; whiskey when you are well, whiskey if you be sick, whiskey almost as soon as you are born, whiskey the last thing before you die – that is Scotland. Whiskey, and that of the crudest and most shuddering quality, is undoubtedly the Scotchman's peculiar vanity. The amount that he can consume without turning a hair is quite appalling. I have seen a Scotchman drink three bottles of Glenlivet on a railway journey from King's Cross to Edinburgh, and when he got out at Edinburgh he strutted doucely to the refreshment bar and demanded further whiskey.'

TWH CROSLAND, *THE UNSPEAKABLE SCOT* (1902).

Crosland was an admirer of the new school of Scottish literary realism, spearheaded by George Douglas Brown's 1901 novel *The House with the Green Shutters*. *The Unspeakable Scot* was his contribution to the reaction against the cosy sentimentality of the 'kailyard' school of Scottish novelists, which included SR Crockett and JM Barrie.

John MacDougall Hay's 1914 novel *Gillespie* takes the 'whisky as devil' theme to new heights. Gillespie Strang's wife, Morag, murders their son, Eoghan, by slashing his throat while hallucinating due to the effects of excessive whisky consumption, and then dies after falling against the fender. Strang subsequently dies from lockjaw, contracted after stepping on glass from one of his late wife's discarded whisky bottles.

It remains an enduring mystery as to why these episodes have never featured in a country & western song.

Whisky fulfills a similar role in one of the great depictions of Scottish urban life *No Mean City* (1935), written by H Kingsley Long and Alexander McArthur. One of the central characters is Johnnie Stark, the 'Razor King' of Glasgow's violent Gorbals during the 1920s, and a man whose spiralling addiction to whisky ultimately costs him his life. He reaches the stage where '…the first swallow of whisky made him feel sick again, but another gulp steadied him and put fresh heart into him.' Stark is ultimately kicked to death in a fight after whisky has clouded his judgment.

'I don't mind your ritzing me or drinking your lunch out of a Scotch bottle. I don't mind your showing me your legs. They're very swell legs and it's a pleasure to make their acquaintance. I don't mind if you don't like my manners. They're pretty bad. I grieve over them during the long winter evenings.'

RAYMOND CHANDLER, *THE BIG SLEEP* (1939).

'I would rather have been cold sober, but I wasn't. If the night held more work for me, I didn't want to go to it with alcohol dying in me. The snifter revived me a lot. I poured more of the King George into a flask, pocketed it, and went down to a taxi.'

DASHIELL HAMMETT, *RED HARVEST* (1929).

The highly influential Edinburgh poet Robert Fergusson, who died insane in 1774 at the tragically young age of 24, wrote in *The Daft Days*:

> O Muse, be kind, and dinna fash us,
> To flee awa' beyont Parnassus,
> Nor seek for Helicon to wash us,
>   That heath'nish spring!
> Wi' Highland whisky scour our hawses,
>   And gar us sing.

Tobias Smollett in *Humphrey Clinker* notes that Highlanders '...regale themselves with whisky; a malt spirit as strong as geneva, which they swallow in great quantities without any signs of inebriation. They are used to it from the cradle, and find it an excellent preservative against the winter cold, which must be extreme on these mountains. I am told that it is given with great success to infants, as a cordial in the confluent smallpox when the eruption seems to flag, and the symptoms grow unfavourable.'

' "How did they lose the license at all?" said Mrs. M'Evoy, "I thought there wasn't a house in Carrow Cross but had one"

' "It was taken from them over some little mistake about selling potheen," replied Dr. Hickey, courteously applying the broken neck of the bottle to Mrs. M'Evoy's tumbler.

' "The police came to search the house, and old Lynch, that was in bed upstairs, heard them, and threw a two-gallon jar of potheen out of the top back window, to break it. The unlucky thing was that there was a goose in the yard, and it was on the goose it fell.'

'The creature!' said Mrs. M'Evoy, 'was she killed?'

'Killed to the bone, as they say,' replied the Doctor, 'but the trouble was, that on account of falling on the goose the jar wasn't broken, so the bobbies got the potheen.'

SOMERVILLE AND ROSS, *THE IRISH RM.*

'It was my Uncle George who discovered that alcohol was a food well in advance of modern medicine.'   PG WODEHOUSE.

Despite many attempts by scientists to artificially speed up the process of maturation without adversely affecting flavour, the best method of producing a decent dram remains that advocated by Russell Sharp. '. ..you fill it into a good oak cask, and you wait 10 or 20 years.'

In *The Dalkey Archive* the great Irish comic novelist Flann O' Brien gives his character De Selby, the mad scientist, a certain advantage when it comes to making good whisky.

'– This is the best whiskey to be had in Ireland, faultlessly made and perfectly matured. I know you will not refuse a taiscaun.

...The water's there, De Selby gestured. Don't steal another man's wife and never water his whiskey. No label on the bottle? True. I made that whiskey myself.

- My dear fellow, De Selby replied, I know all about sherry casks, subterranean repositories and all that extravaganza. But such considerations do not arise here. This whiskey was made last week.

Hackett leaned forward in his chair, startled.

- What was that? he cried. A week old? Then it can't be whiskey at all. Good God, are you trying to give us heart failure or dissolve our kidneys?

...I did not say it was a week old. I said it was made last week.

...I have mastered time. Time has been called, an event, a repository, a continuum, an ingredient of the universe. I can suspend time, negative its apparent course.'

He found that learnin', fame,

Gas, philanthropy, an' steam,

Logic, loyalty, gude name,

    Were a' mere shams;

That the source o' joy below,

An' the antidote to woe,

An' the only proper go,

    Was drinkin' drams.

GEORGE OUTRAM (1805-56).

During the summer of 1803, the poet William Wordsworth and his sister Dorothy made a tour of Scotland. Their adventures were later chronicled in Dorothy's *Recollections of a Tour in Scotland in 1803*.

At Loch Creran the Wordsworths were faced with a dilemma as to what to do with the horse which pulled their Irish jaunting car, as he had earlier misbehaved during a loch crossing, and almost capsized the ferry boat.

'We had determined, whatever it cost, not to trust ourselves with him again in the boat; but sending him round by the lake seemed almost out of the question, there being no road, and probably much difficulty in going round with a horse; so after some deliberation with the ferryman it was agreed that he should swim over. The usual place of ferrying was very broad, but he was led to the point of a peninsula at a little distance. It being an unusual affair, – indeed, the people of the house said that he was the first horse that had ever swum over, – we had several men on board, and the mistress of the house offered herself as an assistant: we supposed for the sake of a share in eighteen-pennyworth of whisky which her husband called for without ceremony, and of which she and the young lasses, who had helped to push the boat into the water, partook as freely as the men.'

Dorothy wrote of Glencoe:

'We parted from our companion at the door of a whisky hovel, a building which, when it came out of the workmen's hands with its unglassed windows, would, in that forlorn region, have been little better than a howling place for the winds, and was now half unroofed. On seeing a smoke, I exclaimed, 'Is it possible any people can live there?' when at least half a dozen, men, women, and children came to the door. They were about to rebuild the hut, and I suppose that they, or some other poor creatures, would dwell there through the winter, dealing out whisky to the starved travellers.'

Dorothy recalled a conversation she had with a guide who accompanied her party from Lanark towards Glasgow:

'I said to him, "How quick you walk!" He replied, "That was not quick walking," and when I asked him what he called so, he said "Five miles an hour," and then related in how many hours he had lately walked from Lanerk [sic] to Edinburgh, done some errands, and returned to Lanerk – I have forgotten the particulars, but it was a very short time – and added that he had an old father who could walk at the rate of four miles and hour, for twenty-four miles, any day, and had never had an hour's sickness in his life. "Then," said I, "he has not drunk much strong liquor?" "Yes, enough to drown him." From his eager manner of uttering this, I inferred that he himself was a drinker; and the man who met us with the car told William that he gained a great deal of money as an errand-goer, but spent it all in tippling.

'I had seen the landlady before we went out, for, as had been usual in all the country inns, there was a demur respecting beds, notwithstanding the house was empty, and there were at least half-a-dozen spare beds. Her countenance corresponded with the unkindness of denying us a fire on a cold night, for she was the most cruel and hateful woman I ever saw. She was overgrown with fat, and was sitting with her feet and legs in a tub of water for the dropsy – probably brought on by whisky-drinking.'

In *Our Man in Havana* the novelist Graham Greene uses whisky miniatures as substitute draughts pieces in a game between the book's hero Wormold, a vacuum-cleaner salesman, and the head of the local Cuban secret police, Segura.

The pieces consist of 12 bourbon miniatures versus 12 Scotch miniatures, and every time a 'piece' is taken, the loser has to drink the contents of the bottle. Wormold wins the game, and Segura passes out, allowing our hero to remove the secret policeman's pistol and extricate himself from a tricky situation.

Greene was a whisky connoisseur and the owner of many miniatures, which he collected during the 1940s and 50s. Eighty of them were auctioned by Christie's in 1994, and rarities in the collection included Donosdale Cream and McCallum's Perfection. The miniatures used in the 1958 film of the novel, starring Alec Guinness and Noel Coward, came from Greene's collection.

The miniatures collected by Greene were about twice the size of their modern counterparts, which meant that a player in the game losing all his pieces would consume well in excess of a full bottle.

With Greene's excellent example in mind, why not play the game at home, perhaps keeping things Scotch and using blends versus malts, with the two players splitting the cost of 'pieces' down the middle. This could become the ultimate Hogmanay pastime for those too miserable or too sensible to go out at New Year. Perhaps some bibulous entrepreneur could even produce a package of the entire game, complete with pieces, board and miniatures of Irn Bru for Ne'er Day's morning...

Malt whiskies are a recurring element in Tom Morton's 1999 novel *Guttered*. The narrator of the book is Zander Flaws, an ex-journalist turned private detective based in Inverness. At the start of the novel the alcoholic Flaws is being lectured by his friend and doctor Cecil 'Hernia' Holdsworth. Holdsworth is, himself, somewhat over-fond of Millburn, produced in Inverness until the distillery's closure in 1985. Flaws takes a drink of Lagavulin from his hip flask during the consultation, noting its aroma of seaweed and peat smoke. 'Then, without warning or hope of control, I threw up, horribly, smokily, peatily, seaweedily.'

> O thou, my Muse! guid auld Scotch drink,
> Whether through wimplin' worms thou jink,
> Or, richly brown, ream o'er the brink,
>   In glorious faem,
> Inspire me, till I lisp and wink,
>   To sing thy name!
>
> ROBERT BURNS (1759-96), *SCOTCH DRINK* (1785).

Scotland, my auld, respected mither!

Tho' whiles ye moistify your leather,

Till whare ye sit on craps o'heather

Ye tine your dam,

Freedom and whisky gang thegither,

Tak aff your dram!

ROBERT BURNS, *THE AUTHOR'S EARNEST CRY AND PRAYER* (1786).

Here's a bottle and an honest friend

What wad ye wish for mair, man?

Wha kens before his life may end,

What his share may be o' care, man?

Then catch the moments as they fly,

And use them as ye ought, man;

Believe me, Happiness is shy,

And comes not aye when sought, man.

ROBERT BURNS, *A BOTTLE AND AN HONEST FRIEND* (1796).

Burns is regarded as the poet of whisky, but Aeneas Macdonald is dismissive of Burns as a connoisseur, believing that he drank 'more for the effect than the flavour', as Neil Gunn wrote of the fisherfolk of his native Caithness.

'Burns, the arch-propogandist of the spirit, was an Ayrshire peasant with a peasant's taste for what was fiery and instant...No word of Burns' gives the slightest impression that he had any interest in the mere bouquet of what he drank; on the contrary, his eloquent praise is lavished on the heating, befuddling effects of whisky.'

This is perhaps not entirely fair, although the whisky drank by Burns would usually have been Lowland spirit – 'rascally liquor' as he called it, from the overworked stills of Kennetpans and its like.

In *Scotch Drink* Burns describes English brandy as 'burning trash', which suggests at least a degree of discrimination.

And as the worth's gane doun, the cost has risen...

And a' that's Scotch aboot it is the name,

Like a'thing else ca'd Scottish nooadays

- A' destitute o' speerit juist the same.

      HUGH MACDIARMID, *A DRUNK MAN LOOKS AT THE THISTLE* (1926).

The long poem *A Drunk Man Looks at the Thistle* is generally considered to be one of the finest works of the most influential figure in twentieth century Scottish literature.

It was typical of the nature of Hugh MacDiarmid that he should 'have little patience with the pseudo-poetical attempts to describe the differences in flavour of the various malts.' It was equally typical that he should believe 'You can only know any or all of them by actually drinking them.'

A modern sculpture of corten steel and bronze in the shape of a giant open book was erected on a hillside overlooking MacDiarmid's birthplace of Langholm in the Borders, after his death in 1978. The sculpture includes symbols relevant to MacDiarmid's life and work, including a pipe and a half-bottle of whisky. When the great poet's widow, Valda, was asked by the sculptor, Jake Harvey, for her opinion of his somewhat unconventional memorial, she expressed one reservation. 'It shouldn't have been a half bottle,' she said.

O it's dowf tae be drinkan alane, my luve,

Whan I wud drink wi my dear,

Nor Crabbie nor Bell's can fire me, luve,

As they wud an you were here.

SYDNEY GOODSIR SMITH, *THE STEEPLE BAR, PERTH*

(FROM *COLLECTED POEMS*, 1975).

Along with Hugh McDiarmid, Sydney Goodsir Smith was one of the leading figures in the Scottish literary renaisance, and one of the Edinburgh 'Pub Poets' who frequented the many bars to be found in the capital's Rose Street. Norman McCaig could sometimes be found in his company.

The Envoi to MacCaig's *Ballade of Good Whisky* (from *A Round of Applause*, 1962) is addressed to Hugh MacDiarmid's real name Christopher Murray Grieve.

Chris! (whether perpendicular or flat

Or moving rather horribly aslant)

Here is a toast that you won't scunner at:

Glenfiddich, Bruichladdich and Glengrant!

Burns Suppers have always provided a good excuse for excessive conviviality. Not to drink vast quantities of whisky during them would be an insult to the Bard and his appreciation for the National Drink. Or so many bekilted and befuddled husbands have insisted to their wives in the early hours of January mornings.

JG Lockhart wrote in *Peter's Letters to his Kinsfolk* (1819) of attending a Burns Supper in Edinburgh at which the literary luminaries John Wilson and James Hogg were also present.

'I was placed within a few feet of Hogg, and introduced to Wilson across the table, and soon found, from the way in which the bottle circulated in this quarter, that both of them inherited in perfection the old feud of Burns against the 'aquae potores'. As to the bottle, indeed, I should exclude Hogg; for he, long before I came into his neighbourhood, had finished the bottle of port allowed by our traiteur, and was deep in a huge jug of whisky toddy – in the manufacture of which he is supposed to excel almost as much as Burns did – and in its consumption too, although happily in rather a more moderate degree.'

Juvenis: 'Jolly day we had last week at McFoggarty's wedding! Capital champagne he gave us, a nd we did it justice, I can tell you –'.

Senex (who prefers whisky): 'Eh–h, mun, it's a' vera weel weddings at ye-er time o' life. Gie me a gude solid funeral!'

Chapter 6
Dying for it

Whisky has long been an essential component of Scottish funerals, providing solace in time of loss and acting as a 'bracer' to help the mourners through the traumas of the occasion. It has also been consumed in large quantities on the sometimes dubious grounds that 'Wullie could have wanted it this way.'

Tobias Smollett wrote in his novel, *Humphrey Clinker* (1771):

'Yesterday we were invited to the funeral of an old lady...and found ourselves in the midst of fifty people, who were regaled with a sumptuous feast, accompanied with the music of a dozen pipers. In short, this meeting had all the air of a grand festival; and the guests did such honour to the entertainment, that many of them could not stand when they were reminded of the business on which we had met. The company forthwith taking horse, rode in a very irregular cavalcade to the place of interment, a church, at the distance of two long miles from the castle. On our arrival, however, we found that we had committed a small oversight, in leaving the corpse behind; so that we were obliged to wheel about, and met the old woman half-way, carried upon poles by the nearest relations of her family...The body was committed to the earth, the pipers playing a pibroch all the time, and all the company standing uncovered. The ceremony was closed with the discharge of pistols; then we returned to castle, resumed the bottle, and by midnight there was not a sober person in the family, the females excepted...Our entertainer was a little chagrined at our retreat, and afterwards seemed to think it a disparagement to his family, that not above an hundred gallons of whisky had been drank upon such a solemn occasion. This morning we got up by four to hunt the roebuck...'

Forgetting the corpse was not just something that happened in eighteenth century fiction. James Ross recounts the following story of a funeral of an old lady on an Outer Hebridean island early in the twentieth century: '...the rather high-spirited company set off with the empty coffin, commenting to each other that Margaret must have wasted away a lot during her last illness. They buried the coffin with all ceremony and returned to the house of mourning to find old Margaret's body still stretched out and awaiting burial.'

Sometimes, of course, facts are not allowed to stand in the way of a good legend. One example is the funeral of John Campbell, Chamberlain to the Duke of Argyll, which took place on Islay in September 1872. Campbell's body was transported by steamer from his home on Mull to Kildalton on the south-eastern shore of Islay for burial, and according to the story that has come down through the years, his coffin was accidentally mislaid between Port Ellen and the cemetery on account of the number of 'dram breaks' which were taken by the bearers and assembled mourners.

A version closer to the truth is to be found in a letter from John Campbell's nephew, Archibald, to his daughter, Jose. Archibald Campbell noted that, 'By 6 o' clock a.m. about 25 relations and friends were assembled at a sumptuous breakfast − in relays − over which I presided, but could not join in, chops, eggs, cakes, Ham, pies all disappeared in a marvellous manner and in almost solemn silence, at the same time the whole of the Duke's tenants − about 150 − had assembled outside and we regaled with bread, biscuits, cheese and whiskey − This over we started in procession, the Bier with the longest coffin I ever saw being carried shoulder high by 12 of the tenants who were releived by others at short intervals, on each occasion of changing carriers, these rough looking men on shouldering the Bier sobbed and cried like children and all who understood Gaelic − which embraced all present could hear them muttering regrets for the loss of their best friend, and all agreeing that they should − would − never see his like again. At 9 we reached the new pier near Bunessan built by Uncle where the steamer − *Dunvegan Castle* − had just arrived from Glasgow to take us to Ardmore − The whole throng pressed us to take them to Islay which we could not do but we did take about 60 and at 10 in the most brilliant sunshine and on a smooth sea we started on our mournful errand, steaming down the Sound of Iona, one flag flying half mast high we went on past Colonsay, entered the sound of Islay and at 4 o'clock cast anchor in Ardmore Bay.'

Once the interment was over, the party returned to the steamer, and Campbell wrote, 'We fed the tenants on Bread, Biscuits, cheese, cold roast Mutton, hot Potatoes, Tea and Whiskey and in the cabin we had soup, Lamb, Mutton, Turkey, Chicken pies, Ham, Butter, cheese, jams and now dear Jose and all of you I have given you an account of a Highland Funeral much in the older style, with the single exception of perfect sobriety which Aunt Flora was most anxious to secure and which John MacNicoll and I were determined to maintain and succeeded in doing.'

According to James Ross, 'at the funeral of Fraser of Lovat in 1815, it is said that some of the mourners drank so much that they fell into the vault.'

At another Highland funeral an old retainer refused to allow guests to leave, insisting, 'It was the express will o' the dead that I should fill ye a' fou, and I maun fulfil the will o' the dead.'

The Reverend Charles Rogers noted that '...the funeral expenses of Hugh Campbell of Calder in 1616 amounted to £647 16s 4d. This expenditure included a charge for whisky equal to one-fourth of the amount.'

The story is told of a Highlander, exiled in Edinburgh, who took his newly-deceased mother's body north to the family burial ground. He hired a hearse for the journey, and when he returned his friends were astonished to find the vehicle full of illicit whisky. 'I took away the mortal remains, but I brought back the spirit,' he explained.

A minister was comforting a dying Highlander when he was disturbed to hear the patient ask him if there was any whisky in heaven. 'Ye ken, sir, it's not that I care for it, but it looks well on the table,' he added.

Many people have died drinking whisky, but some have died making it. Donald Johnston of Laphroaig died in June 1847 after falling into a vat of pot ale, while in 1898 William Robertson, head maltman at Glen Grant Distillery in Rothes, fell into a grain store and was suffocated. Six years later a nine-year-old boy died from burns after falling into a washback at Cragganmore.

The record-breaking Glenturret Distillery cat Towser may have his own statue, and may have created a hundred merchandising opportunities, but not all distillery felines have fared so well. One cat in a necessarily anonymous Speyside distillery missed her footing while mousing and tumbled into the mash tun, which was full of extremely hot wort. Unconcerned, the mashman continued with his work, and the animal was duly distilled. We have all drank a 'hair of the dog', but this was surely taking things a bit too far!

A number of distilleries are said to be haunted by ghosts. One example is Glenmorangie, near Tain in the county of Ross-shire, where the 'White Lady' reputedly haunted the old floor maltings. The White Lady was used to advantage by managers of Glenmorangie, who would warn young apprentices when they began work at the distillery that the sight of the apparition had been enough to drive some men mad. Most new apprentices began work on the malting floor, turning 'the piece' as the malting barley was known, and after being warned about the White Lady none of them ever went to sleep on the job, previously a not uncommon experience!

It is claimed that Campbeltown's Glen Scotia Distillery is haunted by the ghost of former proprietor Duncan MacCallum, who committed suicide by drowning himself in nearby Campbeltown Loch in 1930, after being cheated out of a fortune in a crooked business deal.

Speyside seems to be a particularly rich hunting ground for spectres, with Cardhu, Aberlour and Glenrothes all claiming their share of hauntings. The Glenrothes ghost was thought to be that of Biawa Makalanga, the African boy found abandoned by Major James Grant during a hunting trip to Matebeleland in the 1890s, and subsequently brought back to Speyside.

It was not unknown for fake funeral corteges to be used as cover for the transportation of casks of illicit whisky, and the pretence of death could be a useful stratagem for illicit whisky-makers in times of crisis as Alfred Barnard recalled.

'...the site whereon the distillery [Highland Park] now stands was the place where the famous Magnus Eunson carried on his operations.

This man was the greatest and most accomplished smuggler in Orkney. By profession he was a U.P. Church Officer, and kept a stock of illicit whisky under the pulpit, but in reality he was a "non Professing" distiller. This godly person was accustomed to give out the sermons in a more unctuous manner than usual if the excise officers were in church, as he knew that he was suspected, and that a party of the revenue officers, taking advantage of his absence, might at that moment be searching his house. A singular story is told of this man. Hearing that the Church was about to be searched for whisky by a new party of excisemen, Eunson had the kegs all removed to his house, placed in the middle of an empty room, and covered with a clean white cloth. As the officers approached after their unsuccessful search in the church, Eunson gathered all his people, including the maidservants, round the whisky, which, with its covering of white, under which a coffin lid had been placed, looked like a bier. Eunson knelt at the head with the Bible in his hand and the others with their psalm books. As the door opened they set up a wail for the dead, and Eunson made a sign to the officers that it was a death, and one of the attendants whispered "smallpox." Immediately the officer and his men made off as fast as they could, and left the smuggler for some time in peace.'

John Dearg was a smuggler who had grown wealthy on his trade, and acted as a whisky distributor as well as a distiller. One day he was notified that excise officers were in the neighbourhood, at a time when he had a large consignment of illicit spirit ready to be transported to Invergordon. As he was well-known to the gaugers he needed to think of something quickly. A tailor who happened to be in the house was persuaded to pose as a corpse, with a boll of whisky as his reward. He was duly laid out with a sheet over him, while the women of the house set up a lamentation and Dearg began to read a psalm from his Bible. When the gaugers knocked at the door the wily tailor said, 'I will call out unless you give me two bolls,' and Dearg was forced to agree. When he opened the door to the gaugers they retreated in embarrassment, having intruded on the recent death of his 'brother'. It was only much later that they discovered John Dearg did not have a brother.

Excisemen lived a very violent life, with many dying in the line of duty. In 1817 a Supervisor of Excise, George Arthur, was killed in a fight with smugglers near Campbeltown, while another officer was shot dead on the Cabrach in Speyside, with a bullet said to have been intended for his horse.

Inevitably, whisky smugglers died during their encounters with excisemen, too, and a number of officers faced murder charges as a result. Not surprisingly, therefore, they were loathe to use firearms to defend themselves unless absolutely necessary.

Malcolm Gillespie was a well-known and fearless excise officer in north-east Scotland, and the subject of the book *Report of the Trial of Malcolm Gillespie for Forgery*.

Gillespie trained a bull-terrier to seize smugglers' horses by their noses to make them rear up and drop their loads. During his short career, the dog had a number of successes, beginning in February 1816 when he caused all four smugglers' horses to lose their loads in an encounter at Midmar Lodge in Aberdeenshire. Just five months later, however, the dog was shot dead by a smuggler near Kintore.

In a statement made before his execution in Aberdeen for forgery on 16th November 1827, Gillespie claimed that he had more than 40 wounds on his body as a direct result of his work for the excise service. During his 28 years with the service Gillespie was responsible for the seizure of no less than 6,535 gallons of whisky, 62,400 gallons of wash (from which whisky was to be distilled), 407 actual stills, and even 85 carts and 165 horses!

'I should never have switched from Scotch to Martinis.'
HUMPHREY BOGART'S LAST WORDS (1957).

Index

(Names in italics refer to brands or titles of books etc)

Whisky, Wit & Wisdom

Whisky – the water of life and one of the world's greatest social lubricants has been around in one form or another for well over 500 years. In that time it has gathered around it a folklore all of its own, and over the course of the last 200 years a body of anecdote, involving tales funny, peculiar and frequently bizarre, has evolved.

"Eh, but I had a rare time last year-r. A was at ma cousin MacWhuskie's a whole forrtnicht, an' A didna once ken A was theer!"

Consider those who have drunk it and had something to say about it. Humphrey Bogart's last words were: 'I should never have switched from Scotch to Martinis.' Or Tommy Dewar who once famously stated, 'We have a great regard for old age when it is bottled.' And he should have known, being one of the famous 'Whisky Barons' of the late 19th and early 20th centuries.

But whisky (in all its forms) has fostered more than anecdote and after-dinner stories. It has created an enormous amount of goodwill around the world and deserves its place at the top table of the truly great spirits. It has also lined the pockets of governments who regard it as a gold mine, something they have always relied upon when revenues dry up elsewhere. So it is only fitting that the whisky drinker has ignored that aspect of whisky's heritage and has managed to create a Pandora's Box of material which Gavin Smith has brought together in this book.

Covering every aspect from making it and drinking it, through banning it and selling it, to writing about it and dying for it, Smith has meticulously collated a wealth of stories and facts which confirm what all lovers of Scotch have always known...there is nothing quite like it.

So pour a dram, drop into your favourite armchair and indulge yourself in some *Whisky, Wit & Wisdom*. And whatever you do, don't do what Bogey did!

GAVIN D. SMITH is a freelance journalist and autho specialising in horseracing and whisky. He is the author o *Scotch Whisky*, the *A-Z of Whisky* and co-author of *Wor Worms & Washbacks – Memoirs From the Stillhouse* with John MacDougall. He is married and lives in Perth.

ISBN 1- 897784- 90-2
RRP: £7.99

Angels Share

ISBN 1-897784-90-2

9 781897 784907

06-DOB-214